Illegitimate:

Trump's Election and Failed Presidency

Harold J. Breaux

Editor: Deborah Kevin
Cover Design: Hanne Brøter of Your Brand Vision
Interior Layout: Catherine Williams of Chapter One Book Production

ISBN 978-0-578-74867-2

Dedication to Nollie J. Arcement Jr.

Teacher, Mentor, Coach, and Lifetime Friend

I grew up in an Acadian community in Louisiana, in incredible poverty, but in a nurturing community of grandparents, aunts, uncles, cousins, and friends. And then there were my teachers who early on thought that I had potential with so many of them taking a special interest in helping me to overcome the poverty of my surroundings. In high school, Nollie Arcement was my homeroom teacher, American history teacher, and track coach. I trace my early interest in American history and current events to him. His American history class was a discussion where all classroom students were enticed and invigorated to participate. In my senior year, Nollie took me aside and broached the subject of college, to which I had given little thought. My father and mother had completed the fourth and sixth grades, respectively, and had no money whatsoever for college. As we talked, I was somewhat ambivalent about any college plans. Nollie eventually said, *"You are going to college, or I'll kick your butt."* Then he put his arm around my shoulder and said: "Let's go talk some more." We spoke, and the rest is history.

Over the decades, when I occasionally flew home to my native Louisiana, an early visit and lunch with Nollie were high on my agenda. Having moved to Maryland after college, I look back with regret at not having made more frequent contact with this dear man. Nollie eventually became a Lafourche Parish school supervisor and deputy superintendent of schools. His early work on establishing the first track and field program in our Raceland High School (we won district championships in the first two years of the newly established program) and his continued efforts on promoting track and field in Lafourche Parish led to the Lafourche Parish school system naming an annual regional area track meet as "The Nollie Arcement Relays"—a small tribute to this great man.

Table of Contents

Preface

I am not a professional journalist, politician, or otherwise one who typically writes books about presidents, presidential candidates, or other major public figures and related elections. However, I have long had a keen lifetime interest in daily following essential issues and developments nationally (within the United States) and internationally. This includes daily reading of numerous news and opinion journals, newspapers, books, and watching major news and commentary on TV, following daily events and issues with a particular focus in recent years on events and issues leading to Trump's election and his performance in office. In the process, I have routinely written comments to the author of an article, (in particular, on the Trump presidency) that I particularly liked or disliked.

My background is that of a United States Army commissioned officer (through ROTC), a long career as a Department of the Army/Defense Department civil servant, a B.S. in Physics, a Master of Applied Sciences (focusing on mathematics, engineering, and computer science) with extensive additional Ph.D. level graduate studies beyond the masters. Early in my professional life, I became a ballistician involved with mathematics, physics, and computer science governing and predicting the flight of missiles and shells that were integrated into the fire control mathematics in weapons systems such as the Apache and Cobra helicopters and the Lance and Advanced Pershing nuclear missiles. Later in my career, I performed extensive research on the feasibility of laser weapons focusing on high energy laser propagation and effects—a technology that has now come to fruition in the Army, Navy, and Air Force.

My career spanned fifty years, two as an Army officer, thirty-three as a civilian employee, initially working the technologies described above, and finally, in a significant managerial role in the Army and Defense Department effort to acquire, network, exploit, and provide supercomputers to defense scientists across the country. This thirty-five-year career was followed by a fifteen-year consulting agreement with the Army on super-computer technology and exploitation.

The tasks I faced continually required the search for new and improved means for addressing challenging problems by a methodology that was either new or otherwise not routinely employed for the specific tasks. As a result, I was consistently faced with analyzing difficult issues for which the solution required either developing or adapting unique, complex mathematical methodology. In retirement, I naturally gravitated to examining various issues from the perspective of my background, i.e., through the insight that might be provided by mathematical modeling using the skills honed over my career.

Early in retirement, I became interested in a local Harford County, Maryland issue that concerned the yearly increase in funding needed to pay for salaries for the local sheriff's department and schoolteachers. Through the insight provided by mathematics, I became convinced that officials responsible for the budget were grossly overestimating these costs–a fact that led to the county's consistently withholding incentive pay for experience (so-called experience increments) leading to a loss of experienced personnel to nearby counties. Through mathematics, I proved the point and made a PowerPoint presentation to the County Board of Education.

In the process, I discovered that the issue I addressed was common throughout the country and was derived from what I called a "logical mind trap." In seeking to provide the benefit of my analysis to a broad community, I began and placed the results on a blog at www.complexpolitics.wordpress.com. The effort was successful in that the county school system, after that, provided "catch up" increments in the pay structure for the county's teachers.

After the presidential election of 2016, I became interested in how the Electoral College led to the election of Donald Trump as president, despite his losing the popular vote by nearly three million votes. My interest in the topic led to my writing, in January 2018, a thirty-page paper for my above-listed blog titled, "Mathematics of a Triple Whammy: How the Combination of the Comey Letter, Voter Suppression, and Fake News Tilted Michigan, Wisconsin, and Pennsylvania and the Electoral College to Trump." The idea for this book originated as a revision and extension of that paper.

The election of 2016 will remain of great historical interest and, as a result, has been examined and written about regarding both the Comey Letter and fake news (domestic and Russian). In addition to applying mathematics to these two topics, this book examines in depth the additional whammy associated with voter suppression.

Regarding the election of 2016 outcome, there remain many naysayers, including President Trump, who deny the fundamental claim made in this book that Trump's election was illegitimate. By contrast, as the impeachment hearings proceeded in 2020, one continually found many examples of commentary that Trump's detractors had the objective of removing a "duly elected president." Most interestingly, Webster's lists the words "duly elected official" as the most common usage of the word "duly" with synonyms listed as "correctly, fittingly, properly, and rightly." By contrast,

Webster's lists several of the most common antonyms to "duly" as "unacceptable, unsatisfactorily, and inappropriate." These definitions, analysis of nefarious tactics employed, and the mathematical analysis of the effects of the three "whammies" and how they convincingly tilted the three swing states of Michigan, Wisconsin, and Pennsylvania, and the Electoral College, are a major portion of this book.

The goal of this book is to contribute a further understanding (and hopefully helping to assure hereafter) of how, in the words of MSNBC's Morning Joe host, ex-Republican Congressman Joe Scarborough, Trump's election was, "A Once in a Lifetime Anomaly."

Introduction

Elections experience events that work for or against competing candidates. Some of these events can be pivotal or thought to be so, in changing the projected winner. Pre-election polls continually monitor the standing of the candidates and serve as fodder for pundits to speculate, analyze, and conclude how these events affected the election outcome. This was especially true in the aftermath of the presidential election of 2016. Some of these events were driven by tactics or stumbles of the candidates themselves, but other events were beyond the involvement or creation by any of the competing candidates. Regardless of the origin of these events, it is normal for post-election pundits to examine the postmortems of the campaigns with particular emphasis on such potentially pivotal events that are perceived to have caused a significant shift in votes as measured by polls.

One of the most notorious events of the type described above that occurred in the 2016 election is that associated with the last-minute FBI Comey Letter to Congress described in Chapter 2. This book seeks to advance the state of analysis of such game-changing events beyond the analytical tools used by the famed poll analyst, Nate Silver, in his analysis of the Comey Letter effect. In addition, this book will examine at length the impact of voter suppression and fake news/Russian meddling. A focus will be placed on the analysis of vote switching in the context of two dominant competing contestants with third-party candidates drawing votes, the number which is significant in comparison to the otherwise small margins between the two leading candidates. The importance of this extension is the following.

Vote switching occurring between the two dominant candidates have a doubling effect, i.e., if candidate A loses L votes to candidate B, the difference in vote totals between the two candidates is 2 L. Alternatively, if candidate A loses L votes to third-parties, his/her loss relative to candidate B is only L votes. Most elections and vote switching events lead to some combination of both of these types of vote switching, which in turn adds another variable to the dynamic, namely the fraction z that switched to third parties with the remaining fraction 1 -z switching to the dominant competitor.

Given that exceedingly small margins determined the election of 2016, any analysis not evaluating this latter factor is incomplete. This necessitates the refinement of analytical tools in the form of simple formulas that are developed in this book.

Chapter 1 will describe what we knew or should have known about Trump before the election. Chapter 2 will focus on the Comey Letter; Chapter 3 will examine the effect of voter suppression, and Chapter 4 will examine the effect of fake news/ Russian meddling. The author has labeled these three events as "whammies"(devastating setbacks), which led to voting switches or vote prevention and defined a mathematical term called the Maximum Whammy Effect (MWE). In conjunction with the MWE, I defined a term or variable as the Tilt Margin, TM, which is defined as the number of votes required to tilt the election to or away from one candidate or the other. Given the description above of how vote switching has a doubling effect or a one to one effect, depending on third parties, the structure of MWE and TM is constructed to include the variable z and the fractional distribution of vote switching between dominant candidates versus that involving third parties. These two dominant variables, MWE and TM are combined into a third quantity–the Maximum Whammy Effect Ratio (MWER) equal to MWE/TM. The utility of this structure is the following. If MWER exceeds 1.0, then one concludes that the MWE effect, namely the event associated with that whammy, led to vote switching of a magnitude that tilted the election.

Regarding the 2016 election, it will be shown that MWER, for some whammies, was so much greater than 1.0 that it is easy to conclude the source(s) or events leading to Trump's victory and Clinton's loss. Because of the self-consistent base of reference concerning the three whammies, it is easy and natural to sum the three MWER values and thus easily make conclusions on their total effect on tilting the election to Trump. The definition and details of the structure of these key variables, MWE, TM, z, and MWEM, are derived in Appendix I of this book.

This book goes beyond that analysis described above. Chapter 5 describes Trump's obsession with his predecessor, President Barack Obama. Chapter 6 describes Trump's most unusual penchant for lying on matters big and small and his historical admission, in his first book, that he did so routinely for its effect on his perceived stature. Chapter 7 describes his biggest and most consequential failure, his failure to provide an effective national response to the pandemic of COVID-19.

The publication of the book *Fire and Fury* by Michael Wolff[1] in 2018 heightened the national angst over the first year of the presidency of Donald Trump, angst that has been further heightened since then. This associated fury and national angst includes the natural question, "how did this presidency occur?"

An aspect of this intense focus is that the die has been cast for historians and political scientists to address the question far into the future. This book is the author's effort to address and answer that question. There is little doubt that the answer lies through a quirk associated with the Electoral College, provided by the *triple whammy:*

- The FBI James Comey October 28, 2016, letter to Congress
- Republican-driven voter suppression; and
- Fake news:
    - Domestic fake news circulated through social media; and
    - Russian-driven fake news and meddling.

After the three states of Michigan, Wisconsin, and Pennsylvania (hereafter referred to as MWP) provided the winning margin in the anachronistic Electoral College,[2] Trump[3] erroneously claimed it "was the greatest since Ronald Reagan."

The primary historical question is thus: What were the vote swings from Clinton and fringe candidates to Trump caused by each of these three "whammies?" Numerous books have been written examining the intrigue of the campaign associated with the 2016 presidential election, its outcome (decided by the Electoral College), and the Trump administration performance in office.

In 2018, Lanny Davis published a book titled *The Unmaking of the President 2016.*[4] The Introduction of Davis' book was titled "The Illegitimate President." Davis' primary focus was on the effect of the Comey Letter where he employed analysis by Silver, described above, to include the Small (1%) and Large (4%) Comey Letter effects. His analysis included an extensive rebuttal of claims that suggested other factors (other than the Comey Letter) caused the Clinton loss. Like Silver, Davis made no accounting of the inherent vote doubling factor nor of the adjustments in modeling necessitated by third party effects.

Malcolm Nance, a cybersecurity expert, wrote *The Plot to Hack America*,[5] which was published before the election. In his book, Nance provides an expert look at the inner workings of the Russian intelligence apparatus and how it was structured and operated to swing the then on-going election to Donald Trump. In 2019, Nance followed up with a book titled *The Plot to Betray America: How Team Trump Embraced Our Enemies, Compromised Our Security, and How We Can Fix It.*[6] In 2018, Kathleen Hall Jamieson, a university professor, published *Cyber Wars: How Russian Hackers and Trolls Helped Elect a President.*[7] Jamieson's hesitancy, in her book, (and reluctance to conclude) that the Russian effort was determinant in Trump's election win is exemplified in her book subtitle *What We Don't, Can't and Do Know.* However, in a published interview[8] with Jane Meyer of the *New Yorker,* Jamieson was asked point-blank if she thought that Trump would be president without the aid of Russians, and she didn't equivocate. "No," she said, smiling.

One of the topics gaining the least analysis, except for the work of Greg Palast,[9,10] which will be utilized extensively herein, is a detailed analysis of the question of voter suppression—a factor which this book will seek to cover in-depth. In the many publications, a second omission (or at best an incomplete treatment) is how the totality, or sum, of the various factors analyzed in this book, individually and collectively led to Trump's Electoral College win by his margins in the three battleground states of Michigan, Wisconsin, and Pennsylvania. The point is that one might examine individual components (as done herein) of the three whammies and conclude for history that it might (or might not) seem to be conclusive (as a single entity) to have been pivotal or determinant in tilting the election. It will be shown in this book that all three whammies were nefarious, not acceptable occurrences or tactics for an election.

The Comey Letter alone was pivotal/determinant in all three states. Voter suppression was pivotal/determinant in both Michigan and Wisconsin. The combination of voter suppression and fake news/Russian meddling was pivotal/determinant in Pennsylvania. Whether fake news/Russian meddling, as a single whammy, was itself pivotal/determinant is subject to unresolved issues of persuasion and exposure rates. This book extends the analysis on this latter component through a parametric analysis that helps to understand the jeopardy that fake news/Russian meddling poses to the integrity of our elections.

Should one conclude, despite the analysis herein, that an individual whammy was not pivotal when analyzed alone, nevertheless, when taken together, little or no doubt should remain that the total effect led to this illegitimate presidency. The mathematical formulation developed in this book provides a very convenient, self-consistent structure to examine these additive effects.

As of this writing, the drama associated with the official findings of the Mueller commission, Congressional discussions and impeachment actions, and the court battles between the president and Congress over information gathering relative to campaign intrigue (before and after the 2016 election), tax returns, and strategies to contain COVID-19 remains in full swing.

Numerous articles and books have been written describing specific, single, or individual components of the triple whammy and the likely effect on Trump's margin in MWP and how these three states tilted the Electoral College. In an article titled, "How to Hijack an Election," deBuys[11] addresses these factors in a generalized description, but his lack of any numerical accounting allows the issue to fester without any definitive conclusion (aggravated by Trump's tweets about the brilliance of his victory). This book goes beyond deBuy's analysis by examining, gleaning, and coalescing facts and data from various research studies on each of the three components and then showing, with detailed mathematical accounting, how the aggregate vote impact of the three, individually and collectively, in each MWP state, compared with and/or exceeded Trump's MWP margins—and thus led to his gaining the presidency.

Trump's view of the Electoral College is memorialized by Abadi:[12]

> However, back in 2012, Trump was denouncing the very system that would eventually hand him the presidency. It was election night, and for a brief time, it seemed that Republican nominee Mitt Romney might win the popular vote over Barack Obama, while still losing the electoral vote.

Abadi lists the Trump tweetstorm that ensued in this interim:

- "The Electoral College is a disaster for a democracy."
- "This election is a total sham and a travesty. We are not a democracy!"
- "He lost the popular vote by a lot and won the election. We should have a revolution in this country." This tweet was later deleted.
- "More votes equals a loss … revolution!"
- "The phoney (sic) Electoral College made a laughingstock out of our nation. The loser one (sic)!"

Romney's early lead in the popular vote did not hold up, and Obama eventually won with 51.1% of the vote. The president was later to reaffirm this position on CBS *60 Minutes* in November 2016 by saying:

> I would rather see it, where you went with simple votes. You know you get 90 million votes. And somebody gets...You know, you get 100 million votes, and somebody gets 90 million votes, and you win. There's a reason for doing this. Because it brings all the states into play.

As is his custom, Trump was later to flip flop on this view when he tweeted his preference to electing a president by the Electoral College by tweeting that "the brilliance of the Electoral College is that you must go to many states to win."

Reflecting on this Trump tweet, it is interesting to note the revelation[13] that the Trump reelection campaign has put in place a substantial multi-state task force to invigorate potential non-voting Trump supporters to register—with the effort geared explicitly to a dozen battleground states such as Florida, Michigan, Wisconsin, and Pennsylvania. In other words, the key, and the aim, is to reelect Trump by the anachronistic Electoral College, not by going to and campaigning in many states (as Trump once suggested), but to focus on the Electoral College and the "battleground states" and replicating the election results of 2016.

Observing this initiative, and Trump and the Senate's inaction on Russian meddling, it is evident to this writer that the 2020 election will again face the following three major issues:

- Voter suppression
- Domestic fake news through social media; and

- Russian (and other countries) fake news and meddling as reported by the Muller commission and the various FBI and US intelligence services.

Given the need to avoid the damage to our democracy that would be caused by a second term Trump presidency (but also as a continuing measure), we need to understand these three issues and seek to remove or minimize their stain on our election process.

Chapter 1

What We Knew (or Should Have Known) About Trump Before the 2016 Election

1-1. Trump's Qualifications to be President

Franklin Roosevelt had been governor of New York before being elected president. Harry Truman had been a US senator and vice president. General Dwight Eisenhower had been supreme allied commander in Europe, leading the United States and its allies to victory over Hitler and the Nazis in WWII. John F. Kennedy had been a WWII hero, author of *Profiles in Courage* (a best-selling book), and senator from Massachusetts. Lyndon Johnson had been a senator from Texas, senate majority leader, and vice president. Richard Nixon had been a senator from California and vice president. George Herbert Walker Bush had been a congressman, CIA director, ambassador to the UN, vice president of the United States before becoming president. Jimmy Carter, a Naval Academy graduate, had been a submarine officer and governor of the state of Georgia. Ronald Reagan had been president of the Screen Actors Guild and governor of California. Bill Clinton had been governor of Arkansas. George W. Bush had been governor of Texas. Barack Obama graduated magna cum laude from Harvard Law School, was the first African American editor of the *Harvard Law Review*, a three-time Illinois Senate member, and US senator from Illinois.

Unsuccessful presidential candidates include Hubert Humphrey, who had been a senator from Minnesota and vice president of the United States. Al Gore was a military officer, had authored a book, titled *Earth in the Balance*, as an early visionary on the need to care for the earth's climate (which eventually led to his winning a Nobel prize), and an originator of key legislation that led to Mosaic (the first internet browser) and the National Research and Education Network (NREN) (both crucial steps leading to the internet as we know it), a senator from Tennessee, and vice president. John Kerry had been a Vietnam war hero, lieutenant governor of Massachusetts, a United States senator, member of the Senate Foreign Relations Committee, and secretary of state.

From these two lists, one can conclude that experience in government and leadership has historically been a bell-weather credential upon which US citizenry bestowed their trust to be their president or serious candidates for the office. And so, in 2016, Donald Trump was elected president of the United States (through the Electoral College) despite losing the popular vote by 2.9 million votes, over a candidate who had been a children and civil rights advocate, an attorney staff member on the Watergate Committee that began the Richard Nixon impeachment process, a United States senator from New York, and US secretary of state.

And so, one might logically ask, what were Donald Trump's credentials? We knew he was a TV program host and were told (especially by him) that he was a highly successful (self-made) businessman who was worth billions of dollars—a much-disputed claim that will be re-examined herein.

One of the tragedies of the 2016 election dynamics was that the Pulitzer Prize-winning journalist, David Kay Johnston,[14] had a late start in writing and publishing his book *The Making of Donald Trump.*

The book was published on July 31, 2016, and, accordingly, there wasn't much time for it to circulate broadly before election day on November 8, 2016. In his book, Johnston states:

> I will always wonder what might have happened had journalists, and some of the sixteen candidates vying with Trump for the Republican nomination, started asking my questions earlier.

In his book Introduction, Johnston summarizes Trump with the words:

> More important, Trump has worked just as hard to make sure few people know about his lifelong entanglements with a major cocaine trafficker, with mobsters and many mob associates, with con artists and swindlers. He has been sued thousands of times for refusing to pay employees, vendors, and others. Investors have sued him for fraud in a number of different cities. But among Trump's most highly refined skills is his ability to deflect or shut down law enforcement investigations.

As I first wrote this quote (namely, sued thousands of times) from Johnston, I noted that it needed to be verified (such a large number of lawsuits seemed incredible) and that it was a possible exaggeration. Later in my research, I found and obtained the book by Zirin titled *Plaintiff in Chief – A Portrait of Donald Trump in 3500 Lawsuits*[15] published in September 2019. This book was thus not available to the voting public before the election in the fall of 2016. However, my research led to finding that on June 16, 2016, four and a half months before the election, *USA Today* published an article titled:[16] "Exclusive: Trump's 3,500 lawsuits: unprecedented for a presidential nominee."

Here one should note that *USA Today* is distributed throughout the United States and has the largest circulation of any newspaper equaling the combined circulation of *the New York Times* and the *Wall Street Journal*. Accordingly, one can conclude that Trump's incredible litigiousness should have been well known. Referring to Trump's lawsuits, the two authors, Penzenstadler and Page, in the *USA Today* article, observed:

> The legal actions provide clues to the leadership style the billionaire businessman would bring to bear as commander in chief. He sometimes responds to even small disputes with overwhelming legal force ... He sometimes refuses to pay real estate brokers, lawyers, and vendors.

Their description of the myriad of Trump lawsuits included the following:

- The sheer volume of lawsuits is unprecedented for a presidential nominee.
- Since his announced candidacy, a year ago, at least seventy new cases have been filed about evenly divided between suits filed by him and his companies and those filed against them.
- He doesn't hesitate to deploy his wealth and legal firepower against adversaries with limited resources, such as homeowners.
- He sometimes refuses to pay real estate brokers, lawyers, and other vendors.
- He also uses the legal system to haggle over his property tax bills.

- His companies have been involved in more than 100 tax disputes, and the New York State Department of Finance has obtained liens on Trump properties for unpaid tax bills at least three dozen times.
- Despite his boasts on the campaign trail that he "never" settles lawsuits, for fear of encouraging more, he and his businesses have settled with plaintiffs in at least 100 cases reviewed by *USA Today.*
- The analysis found Trump has been involved in more legal skirmishes than the next five top real estate companies (of similar size and business) combined.
- Trump railed against a federal judge overseeing a then-ongoing lawsuit against Trump University, saying Judge Gonzalo Curiel "happens to be, we believe, Mexican" and called him a "hater of Donald Trump" who "railroaded" him.
- At times, he and his companies refuse to pay even relatively small bills.
- The *USA Today* analysis identified at least 3,500 legal actions involving Trump.
- Dozens dealt with the bankruptcy of Trump's companies, and dozens more involved plaintiffs' lawsuits against Trump businesses that judges terminated because the Trump companies targeted had gone bankrupt.
- Trump is ... quick to distance himself from deals that struggle, willing to deploy outsized resources against adversaries..., even in disputes that involve small amounts of money ... approaches however appropriate in a business setting may not translate to a political one, especially at the level of the White House.
- Trump distances himself from deals that sour.

- Experts in the presidency say Trump's record ... raises questions about whether he has exhibited the leadership qualities that have distinguished the nation's most successful presidents ... including attention to detail, the subordination of one's ego, and the art of compromise.
- Six in ten voters said they had reservations about or were uncomfortable with Trump's lack of experience in government or the military.

The contradiction in the origin of Trump's wealth and his explanation of why he refused to reveal his tax returns, which he promised to do during the run-up to the election, is examined by Chris Cillizza[17] in a *YouTube* "The Point" video segment.

As noted above, Johnston's book was too late for the tutorial on Trumps' business acumen (or lack thereof) to be fully exposed to the American media and electorate as a whole. As the election of November 2020 approaches, my objective is thus to assist in the national exposure on the following:

- The con job Trump perpetrated on the American public as to his alleged incredible success as a businessman and his myriad of other shortcomings as a candidate.
- A mathematical/statistical analysis of the politics, intrigue, skullduggery, and numbers associated with the three factors (whammies) that made Trump "an illegitimate, unduly elected president."
- Trump's extreme failure as president.

Numerous facets of Trump's history will be examined from listed references that (where available) are dated before November 8, 2016—thus suggesting that the material was available to voters before the 2016 election. Additionally, each sub-topic on Trump's history will also be illuminated further, with cited references that were published after the 2016 election.

1-2. Did Trump Make Billions in Business?

Trump has effectively claimed numerous times that [18] "his success in business was based on getting a one million dollar loan from his father which he had to pay back with interest."

Despite this claim being debunked before the election, the public largely believed it and this belief, undoubtedly, in no small measure, led to his election. Trump became head of his father's real estate empire in 1971. Matthews[19] quotes an article from the *National Journal*:

> ... in 1974, the real estate empire of Trump's father, Fred, was worth about $200 million, making his stake (as one of five siblings) at that time worth about $40 million. If one were to invest $40 million in an S&P index in August of 1974, reinvest all dividends, not cash out and have to pay capital gains, and pay nothing in investment fees, he'd wind up with about $3.4 billion come August 2015.

Matthews also claimed (in March 2016) that "Bloomberg currently estimated Trump's net worth at $2.9 billion with *Forbes* estimating it at $4 billion."

The public was repeatedly told of his great success in business and, in general, the people believed it. Before the election, Fisher and Hobson[20] wrote that Trump had, on several occasions, feigned to be John Miller or John Baron, associates of his. Trump pretending to be John Baron or John Miller, regaled reporters on the phone about his boss (Trump's) relationships with model Marla Maples,

Italian model Carla Bruni, Madonna, and actress Kim Bassinger. Fisher and Hobson reported that "editors at New York tabloids said calls from Trump (posing as Baron) were at points so common that they became a recurring joke on the city desk." Trump was later to name his son with Melania "Barron." Unfortunately, it was not until 2018 that Jonathan Greenberg[21] wrote that, in May 1984, when he was working for *Forbes*, he had been conned by Trump, again posing as John Baron. The latter duped him into believing that Trump's finances were of such a value as to be placed in the *Forbes* 400. Greenberg wrote:

> But it took decades to unwind the elaborate farce Trump had enacted to project an image as one of the richest people in America. Nearly every assertion supporting that claim was untrue. Trump wasn't just poorer than he said he was. Over time, I have learned that he should not have been on the first three *Forbes* 400 lists at all. In our first-ever list, in 1982, we included him at $100 million, but Trump was actually worth roughly $5 million—a paltry sum by the standards of the super-monied peers—as a spate of government reports and books showed only much later.

Many other instances of Trump calling the press posing under pseudonyms are listed by D'Antonio in *Fortune*.[22] Such blatant fostering of "untruths" became a well-known pattern after Trump began his presidency. As a result, the press eventually cast aside its propensity for press manners to replace the word "untruths" with the word "lies" when referring to Trump. In fact, "fact-checking" eventually became a cottage industry, spawned by Trump's lies (as of this writing, more than 16,000, averaging more than ten per day during his presidency).

After the election, the press continued searching for the real value of Trump's finances, the potential violation of the Emoluments Clause, and his potentially steering both the US and foreign government business/funds to his properties. In 2018, Buettner, Craig, and Barstow of *the New York Times* did an extensive investigation into Trump's wealth.[23] One of their findings was that "Trump received the equivalent today of at least $413 million from his father's real estate empire…much of this money came to Mr. Trump through dubious tax schemes."

The New York Times authors listed numerous "takeaways" from *the Times* investigation, including:

- The Trumps' tax maneuvers show a pattern of deception, tax experts say.
- Donald Trump began reaping wealth from his father's real estate empire as a toddler.
- That 'small loan' of one million was actually at least $60.7 million—much of it never repaid.
- Fred Trump wove a safety net that rescued his son from one bad bet after another.
- The Trumps turned an eleven million dollar loan debt into a legally questionable tax write-off.
- Father and son set out to create the myth of a self-made billionaire.
- Donald Trump tried to change his ailing father's will, setting off a family reckoning.
- The Trumps created a company that siphoned cash from the empire.
- The Trump parents dodged hundreds of millions in gift taxes by grossly undervaluing the assets they would pass on.

While this *New York Times* expose appeared in 2018, well after the election, some facets of the findings relative to the Trumps' shady money maneuvers were available to voters before the election. For example, on September 26, 2016, Max Rosenthal of *Mother Jones*[24] quotes from *the Washington Post*'s Michael Kranish and Marc Fisher's book titled *Trump Revealed.*

> The elder Trump sent a lawyer to the Trump Castle to sneak money straight into the casino's coffers. The lawyer, Howard Snyder, approached the casino cage and handed over a certified check for $3.25 million drawn on Fred's account. Snyder then walked over to a Blackjack table where a dealer paid out the entire amount in 670 gray $5,000 chips. The next day the bank wired $150,000 into Fred's account at the Castle, once again Snyder arrived at the casino and collected the full amount in thirty more chips ... Sure enough, the Castle made its bond payment the day Fred's lawyer bought the first batch of chips ... New Jersey's Casino Control Commission investigated the chip purchase the following year and said it was an illegal loan that broke the state's rules about casinos receiving cash from approved financial sources ... In the end, the casino kept the money, and the committee fined the casino the relatively small amount of $65,000.

In summary, the difficulty in assessing Trump's success (or not) is due to his penchant for lying, self-promotion, and ultimately in hiding his income tax returns from the public.

1-3. Trumps are Charged with Discrimination in Housing

Trump's early entry into real estate was as an assistant and heir to his father's business with extensive rental units in New York

City. In 1973, the city sued the Trumps (Donald and father Fred) for housing discrimination because they would not rent apartments in one of their developments to African Americans.[25] A *Washington Post* review of the case[26] describes an abstract from related court documents:

> Two former employees, a husband and wife who rented properties, were quoted in court documents as saying they were told that the company wanted to rent only to 'Jews and executives' and discouraged rental to blacks: The couple told the government's lawyers that they were advised that 'a racial code was in effect, blacks being referred to as 'No. 9.'

The Trumps hired Roy Cohn, the lawyer who had been a top aide to Senator Joseph McCarthy (R-WI) during the communist witch hunt era. The Trumps sued the government for $100 million for falsely accusing them of discrimination. After two years, the case was settled with the agreement prohibiting the Trumps from discriminating and requiring them to acquaint themselves with the Fair Housing Act. The Trumps were required to place ads informing minorities of their equal housing opportunities. Trump declared victory because the deal was completed without acknowledging any wrongdoing.

In 1927, Fred Trump had been arrested at a KKK rally in Jamaica Queens, when 1,000 Klansmen and 100 policemen staged a free-for-all in the streets.[27]

1-4. Trump "Stiffs" Undocumented Polish Workers on the Trump Tower Site

Before erecting the New York City Trump Tower in 1980, the existing building needed to be demolished for the planned replacement. The shenanigans and tactics Trump used on the project turned into a fifteen-year legal battle, the details of which were documented by Calabrese of *Time* on August 25, 2016, before the election. As Trump planned the construction, Calabrese noted:[28]

> It was disgusting how he used people … I said, 'Don't exploit them like that. Don't try to f-ck these poor souls.' It baffled me then and makes me sick even now that he knowingly had these poor souls there for the purpose of Trump Tower at starvation wages. He couldn't give a s-it because he's Donald Trump, and everybody has to serve him. Over time, he became more and more monstrous and arrogant. I asked myself, 'How long is it going to take for all of us to catch up with him?'

It was one of many settlements in Trump's career in which details were not released to the public—and it became a Trump trademark.

1-5. The Donald J. Trump Charitable Foundation (DTCF) was a Scam

The fact that Trump's charity was a scam was known to casual followers of campaign issues in 2016. During the 2016 campaign, Trump engaged in a much-publicized solicitation of funds for veterans' organizations as a substitute for his participation in a Fox debate with other candidates. Corey Lewandowski, a one-time Trump campaign manager, sent an email to the foundation seeking to divert some of these funds, intended for veterans, to the Trump Iowa caucus campaign—a grossly illegal diversion. Only after months of inquiry did the DTCF provide any details on how the veterans' funds were distributed. The New York attorney general later found that some funds had been illegally transferred to pay for expenses related to the Iowa caucus campaign, as Lewandowski had requested.

In September 2016, David Fahrenthold[29] of *the Washington Post* wrote one of several articles which, along with his investigation findings, was to win a Pulitzer Prize later. Fahrenthold described the evolution of the DTCF.

> Trump founded his charity in 1987 and, for years, was its only donor. But in 2006, Trump gave away almost all the money he had donated to the foundation, leaving it with just $4,268 ... The foundation's tax records show no donations from Trump since 2009.

The laws governing the use of charitable foundation funds prohibit "self -dealing," i.e., using the charity's funds to pay for the benefit of the founder and/or the board members of the foundation. Fahrenthold describes several such "self -dealing" payouts by the DJTF to include:

- In 2013, the foundation gave $25,000 to a political group supporting Florida attorney general, Pam Bondi. The gift was made at the time that Bondi's office was considering whether to investigate fraud allegations against Trump University. It didn't. Trump staffers blamed the gift on a clerical error. Later, during the impeachment hearings, Bondi was hired by Trump as one of his defense attorneys.
- In 2012, Trump spent $12,000 of the foundation's money to buy a football helmet signed by then NFL quarterback Tim Tebow.

- In 2007, Trump's wife Melania bid $20,000 for the six-foot-tall portrait of Trump done by a speed painter during a charity gala at Mar-a-Largo. Trump paid for the painting with $20,000 from the foundation.
- In 2006, the Mar-a-Largo club put up a giant American flag on an eighty-foot flagpole. Town rules limited such flagpoles to forty-two feet. After the usual Trump protests and litigation, the town waived $120,000 in fines when Trump gave $120,000 to charities. In Palm Beach, nobody seems to have objected to the penalties assessed on Trump's business being erased by a donation from a charity.
- In 2010, Martin Greenberg hit a hole-in-one in a contest held at Trump's golf course in Westchester, NY, Trump refused to pay the one million dollar prize, saying the shot was one meter short of the mandatory 150 yards, but Trump's club itself had allegedly made the hole too short. Greenberg sued. The Trump Charitable Foundation paid $158,000 to the Martin Greenberg Foundation.
- In 2014, a gala was held at Mar-a-Largo for a children's charity. In an auction of paintings, a four-foot-tall portrait of Trump was purchased for $10,000 and paid for by the Trump foundation. Trump's staff did not respond to questions about where this second painting was displayed. Sharon Anderson, director of the charity, said she had last seen the portrait at Trump's club.

In 2018, the New York State attorney general found[30,31] that the DTCF had committed so many acts of self- dealing that she asked a judge, "To order the Charity to be disbanded, the remaining assets be distributed to other charities and that Trump be forced to pay back at least $2.8 million in restitution and penalties." She asked that Trump be banned from leading any other New York non-profit organization for ten years.

Among numerous malfeasance charges against the DTCF, the attorney general found that three of Trump's children, Don Jr., Eric, and Ivanka, even though they were official board members, had never held a meeting. The Trump Organization treasurer, Allen Weisselberg, who was also officially on the board of the DTCF, denied awareness of being on the board.

Fahrenthold further quotes the New York State attorney general, "The foundation was essentially one of Trump's personal piggybanks—a pool of money that his accounting clerks knew how to use whenever Trump wanted money to pay a non-profit organization."

In November 2019, a New York court handed down a formal decision[32] affirming most of the charges, including two million dollars in restitution.

1-6. Trump Avoided the Draft with a Fake Diagnosis of Bone Spurs

Probably no single factor affects a military veteran's view of a candidate than the reality that a candidate lied about or created a fictitious physical ailment to avoid the draft. History will record precisely that for Donald Trump. Trump had received several draft deferrals while he was in college at Fordham and the University of Pennsylvania. In 1966, Trump was found fit for duty. He had played both baseball and football in college and was eligible for the draft.

During the campaign of 2016, the subject of a possible fake diagnosis surfaced and was denied by Trump. As reported by McMillan,[33] the daughters of recently deceased podiatrist Larry Braunstein told *the New York Times*:

... that their father—as a favor—provided the fall 1968 diagnosis of bone spurs that helped Trump get a medical exemption. In return, the doctor received access to Fred Trump, Trump's father and owner of the Queens' building in which Larry Braunstein's practice operated; If there was anything wrong in the building, my dad would call Trump and Trump would take care of it immediately.

In August 2016, a Howard Stern Interview[34] of Trump was released in which Trump described his sexual relationships with women and the concern about HIV as his "personal Vietnam."

1-7. Birtherism and Trump's Obama Derangement Syndrome

Trump's focus on trashing Barack Obama began with Trump's 2011 claim that Obama was not eligible to be president because he was born in Kenya. In fact, Obama produced both a long-form birth certificate and a newspaper clipping showing that he was born in Honolulu, Hawaii. Only years later was Trump to admit the truth grudgingly but only after falsely blaming Hillary Clinton for having started the birtherism flap. In 2011, Trump went on to belittle Obama's academic record as being unsuitable to be accepted into Harvard. Over time, political scientists will examine whether some of Trump's major initiatives (rollbacks) will have been due to Trump's antipathy toward "all things Obama," including:

- Obamacare
- The six-nation Iran Nuclear Agreement
- The Transpacific Partnership
- Paris Climate Accord, with the US joining Iran and Turkey as the only nonparticipants

- The Nuclear Missile Treaty with Russia
- Deferred Action for Childhood Arrivals DACA
- Abandoning our Kurdish allies in Syria
- Environmental and safety issues

1-8. The Trump University Scandal

As the details of the Trump University Scandal hit the news, Cassidy of the *New Yorker*[35] wrote on June 2, 2016:

> ... the United States is facing a high-stakes social-science experiment. Will one of the world's leading democracies elect as its president a businessman who founded and operated a for-profit learning annex that some of its own employees regarded as a giant rip off, and that the highest legal officer in New York State has described as a classic bait-and-switch scheme?

The so-called Trump University was established in 2005, and the New York State Education Department (NYSED) warned early-on that it violated state law for operating without an NYSED license. When forming the university, Trump's operation ballyhooed the notion that they would hire expert instructors familiar with the tactics and processes that mirrored Trump's real estate successes. In fact, no such experts were ever hired, and most of the students quickly began complaining about the tactics used by the "university" to get students to sign up for more and more extensive and expensive curricula.

Eventually, the complainants joined in a California class-action suit. During the lawsuit, Ronald Schnackenberg, who worked in Trump's office at 40 Wall Street, and is quoted in Cassidy's article, testified that "while Trump University claimed it wanted to help consumers make money in real estate, in fact, Trump University was only interested in selling every person the most expensive seminars they possibly could." The affidavit concluded: "Based on my personal experience and employment, I believe that Trump University was a fraudulent scheme and that it preyed upon the elderly and uneducated to separate them from their money."

In February 2018, a Federal Court in San Francisco approved a twenty-five million dollar settlement in favor of the claimants. After the settlement, Trump tweeted, "The only bad thing about winning the presidency is that I did not have time to go through a long but winning trial on Trump U. Too bad!"

1-9. Trump Claims to be Very Smart—A Very Top Graduate of the University of Pennsylvania Wharton School

Early on, Trump claimed to be an honors and top graduate of the prestigious Wharton School at the University of Pennsylvania. Zarya[36] quotes from a William Geist article in *the New York Times Magazine* in 1984, "the commencement program from 1968 does not list him as graduating with honors of any kind" even though "just about every profile ever written about Mr. Trump states that he graduated first in his class at Wharton in 1968."

Fouhy[37] captures Trump's mendacity by quoting Trump from an Associated Press interview in 2011.

I heard Obama was a terrible student, terrible. How does a bad student go to Columbia and then to Harvard? I'm thinking about it. Let him show his records.

Fouhy continues:

Obama graduated from Columbia University in 1983 with a degree in political science...He went on to Harvard Law School, where he graduated magna cum laude in 1991 and was the first black president of the Harvard Law Review.

The irony of Trump's fixation on things Obama, in this case, Obama's academic record, led to the need to hide his own academic records. Michael Cohen, Trump's former lawyer and "fixer" testified under oath at a Congressional hearing in February 2019, and his testimony is described in *The Philadelphia Inquirer*.[38] Cohen stated that Trump directed him to threaten the president's "high school, his colleges, and the College Board never to release his grades or SAT scores."

The *Inquirer* listed a copy of one of the letters, written under Trump's orders, to Fordham University, a university Trump attended before transferring to Wharton. *The Inquirer* also stated:

A 1973 *New York Times* profile said Trump graduated first in his class from Wharton in 1968. But Trump's name was not included among dean's list students for the 1967-68 school year though it is found on a Penn commencement program from 1968, which lists Trump as graduating from Wharton with a Bachelor of Science in economics.

Fisher[39] wrote that:

In 2011, days after Donald Trump challenged President Barack Obama to 'show his records' to prove that he had not been a 'terrible student,' the headmaster at New York Military Academy got an order from his boss, "Find Trump's academic records and help bury them." The official is reported to have said, "It's the only time I moved an alumnus's records."

An ABC News video[40] is aptly titled, "President Trump has called himself smart six times before January 8, 2018."

Continued, frequent braggadocio about his intellect led to efforts, described by Burleigh of *Newsweek*,[41] to assess and analyze the first 30,000 words spoken by each of the last fifteen presidents after assuming office. The study used the Flesch-Kincaid scale developed in 1976 for the US Navy and more than two dozen other standard tests analyzing English-language difficulty levels. In describing the lexicological analyses, Burleigh states, "Trump came out dead last (mid-fourth-grade level). Trump also uses the fewest unique words (2,605) of any president—Obama was the best at 4,869—and [Trump] uses words with the fewest average syllables."

1-10. Trump: The Bully

In office, President Trump has been notorious for his bullying tactics, tweeting repeated nasty comments at those who cross him, comments which fits Johnston's description of Trump's self-described business practice, "you screw 'em back ten times over."

In 1990, Trump owned development in a casino named the Taj Mahal in Atlantic City, New Jersey, that cost 1.2 billion dollars. It was one of several Trump properties that were later to go down in a string of bankruptcies. Marvin Roffman, a highly respected gaming analyst at the Philadelphia brokerage firm Janney Montgomery Scott, expressed his doubts about the fiscal solvency of the casino to the *Wall Street Journal* in the following words:[42]

> When this property opens, he [Trump] will have so much free publicity, he will break every record in the books in April, June, and July. But once the cold winds blow from October

to February, it won't make it. The market just isn't there ... Atlantic City is an ugly and dreary kind of place. Even its hard-core customers aren't coming down as much.

When Roffman's article appeared in the *Wall Street Journal*, Trump immediately faxed a letter to Janney Chief Executive Norman Wilde expressing his outrage at the quotes, calling Roffman an "unguided missile" and "threatening a major lawsuit unless Mr. Roffman is immediately dismissed or apologizes."

Janney prepared an apology, Roffman withdrew it based on conscience, and Janney fired Roffman. Roffman sued Trump and filed an arbitration claim against Janney. Trump settled for an undisclosed amount, and Roffman won a $750,000 award against Janney. In his usual fashion, Trump unleashed a storm[43] of "screw ems" to various press agencies "calling Roffman a bad analyst, a very unprofessional guy, a totally mediocre guy with no talent, not a good man, and a disgrace to his profession."

As Roffman effectively predicted, the Taj Mahal filed for bankruptcy about a year later and reportedly[44] was sold at four cents on the dollar.

1-11. Trump's Ad Urging Execution of the Central Park Five

In 1989, a big topic in tabloids was the arrest of several teenagers (four black, one Latino) in New York for their alleged rape of a woman in New York City's Central Park. As the trial progressed, Trump paid $65,000 for an ad[45] (described by *the Washington Post*'s Janell Ross) in all four major New York City newspapers urging for, "the need to infringe on the civil liberties of some to protect the law-abiding many ... to reclaim the city from out-of-control groups of criminals and demanded the restoration of the death penalty in New York State."

The five young men were convicted and sentenced to long prison terms. Their sentences were ultimately overturned because four of the five confessions were found to have been coerced. The men were officially exonerated by DNA evidence and a separate confession in 2002 (by an individual matching the DNA evidence). The five were paid $41 million in a 2014 settlement. Ross goes on to observe:

> This week (in October 2016) when confronted again with just how wrong he was about the Central Park Five, Trump not only refused to acknowledge widely reported and well-known facts or the court's official actions in the case. He did not simply refuse to apologize: He described the men as guilty and then demonstrated once again that he is a master of the dark art of using long-standing racial fears, stereotypes, and anxieties to advance his personal and political goals.

1-12. The Access Hollywood Tapes—Teflon Don

The word "Teflon" was originally used as the name of a non-stick coating product developed by Dupont. It has also come into everyday use to describe an individual or event which is impervious, or prone to be unaffected by negative events or circumstances. Trump's relationship to the Access Hollywood Tapes, released on October 7, 2016, a month before the election, will, for all time, characterize Trump as "Teflon Don." The incident was first unearthed by Fahrenthold[46] of *the Washington Post* and has been documented in detail for history by Victor[47] of *the New York Times*, who lists the full transcript. An extract from *the Times* article follows:

> **Mr. Trump**: Yeah, that's her. With the gold. I better use some Tic-Tacs just in case I start kissing her. You know, I'm

automatically attracted to beautiful—I just start kissing them. It's like a magnet. Just kiss. I don't even wait. And when you're a star, they let you do it. You can do anything.
Mr. Bush: Whatever you want.
Mr. Trump: Grab 'em by the pussy. You can do anything.

A video of Trump and Bush departing from a bus and engaging in the conversation is available on YouTube.[48]

Trump apologized, referring to it as "locker room talk," but in the presidential debate the following week, he claimed that Bill Clinton had done far worse and that Hillary Clinton had bullied her husband's victims. Trump paid for and invited several women accusers of Bill Clinton to sit in the front row during the debate.

Billy Bush was fired from his job as a host of the NBC Today show. Senator John McCain said that he would no longer support Trump. Numerous other prominent supporters expressed disapproval, but eventually, their criticism went silent. Like Teflon, Trump seemed to be impervious to the scandal.

1-13. Did Fox Hide News of Hush Money Payments to Stormy Daniels before the Election?

After earlier denials, Michael Cohen, Trump's former attorney, finally admitted in open court that Trump had authorized payment of $130,000 of hush money to porn star Stormy Daniels to hide their alleged affair. Trump, in May 2018, finally admitted to authorizing the payment.[49] The statement appeared to flatly contradict his previous assertion that he was unaware of the payment. The obvious conclusion is that hiding this hush money was viewed as critical to the upcoming election. As reported by Burke,[50] a similar effort, with apparent similar motive, was underway at Fox News as described by Jane Meyer of the *New Yorker*.

Former Fox News reporter Diana Falzone obtained proof of the affair and confirmed it with several key sources, plus reportedly obtained emails between Daniels' attorney and Cohen. According to the *New Yorker*, former Fox News executive Kent LaCorte ultimately told Falzone to, "let it go ... good reporting kiddo, but Rupert [Murdock] wants Donald Trump to win. So just let it go."

And so, I too will always wonder what might have happened had journalists, some of the sixteen candidates vying with Trump for the Republican nomination, and the Hillary Clinton campaign, asked more questions about Trump's history as described in this chapter.

Chapter 2

The First Whammy

2-1. The Letter that Changed the Course of History

Nate Silver, of *Five-Thirty-Eight*, is a famed analyst specializing in the analysis of elections and candidates whose fate is/was conjectured to arise from untoward events such as the Comey Letter. After the 2016 election, Silver wrote ten different articles on the 2016 election featuring the surprising victory of Donald Trump over Hilary Clinton. On November 11, 2016, Silver commented[51] on the possible effect of the Comey Letter, "If there's a late-breaking news-event such as FBI Director James Comey's letter to Congress on October 28, even a 'temporary' effect may still weigh on voters at the time they cast the ballot."

At the time, this was a tentative observation by Silver—not a conclusion. On May 3, 2017, in his tenth article,[52] titled "The Comey Letter Probably Cost Clinton The Election, "he described the press coverage of the Comey Letter.

It was the dominant story of the last ten days of the campaign. According to the news aggregation site Memeorandum, which algorithmically tracks which stories are gaining the most traction in the mainstream media, the Comey Letter was the lead story on six out of seven mornings from October 29 to November 4. In the article, Silver focused on the narrow margins in the three battleground states of Michigan, Wisconsin, and Pennsylvania, the three states that tilted the Electoral College to Trump, despite his losing the popular vote to Clinton by almost three million votes. Silver's analysis is a lengthy examination of poll results in a week or so before the November election, a time when the press and major news outlets intensely covered the topic and its implications. Comey, then FBI director, in his letter to Congress, described the FBI intent to examine the computer and email belonging to ex-Congressman Anthony Weiner, the husband of one of Clinton's staffers named Huma Abedin.

The issue was already toxic because of Clinton's use of a private server for her email and the issue of her alleged erasure of emails. The fact that Weiner was in the news over his alleged sexting of emails to a teenage girl greatly added to this overall toxicity. Two days before the election, Comey, in effect, said, "Oops—there was nothing to the inquiry—no such search was warranted." The damage had been done, and Clinton's standing in the polls plummeted.

Silver's analysis ultimately focused on what he described as the Small Comey Effect (a 1% vote or poll difference), and a Large Comey Effect (a 4% poll difference). Polling data suggested that the Comey Letter had cost Clinton a 2.6% drop in polls nationally and a range of 5-7% in the three MWP states. Silver's analysis was based on showing that smaller percentages than the actual dip in the polls would have tilted the election to Trump. Accordingly, since the percentage losses by Clinton were .78 % in Michigan, .24% in Wisconsin and .72 % in Pennsylvania, these two percentages (1-4%) could then (if the analysis showed them to be pivotal) logically lead to the conclusion that the Comey Effect had tilted the election to Trump.

Lanny Davis is an attorney who has served on important boards under Republican and Democratic presidents but is primarily noted for his association with Democratic Party issues and personnel. In 2018, he published a book[53] titled *The Unmaking of the President 2016*. In this book, Davis describes the Comey Letter event as follows, "The letter was the final event in a sequence that will only gain historical importance and scrutiny in the years ahead ... History and truth require a full accounting."

One of the primary goals of this book is to show that this extensive focus by someone as noted as Silver, followed by the book by Lanny Davis, both doing 1% and 4% (the Small and Large Comey Effect Analysis) provides an incomplete answer to the historical question of the narrowness of the ultimate vote margins that switched the election victory to Trump. This book will show that margins in the range of .39 to .77 percent, (allowing for the vote doubling effects and significant third party effects) in the three MWP swing states explained the difference between a Clinton versus Trump presidency.

During Trump's impeachment hearings, Trump supporters referred to the action as an effort to negate the election of a duly elected president. For these and other reasons, we owe it to history to examine the vote outcome in the three MWP states with as much precision as possible. By establishing that the election was in effect decided by vote switching in MWP by these minuscule percentages should greatly serve to reframe the historical question.

The model used by Silver and Davis can be described as incomplete—in the sense of the assumed poll margins that were analyzed and compared with Trump's winning margin in the MWP states. This book seeks to complete the analysis and overcome the following two shortcomings:

a) No effort was made to determine the minimum percentages necessary for the Comey Letter to have been pivotal.

b) No effort was made to model the margin doubling effect described herein, and the effect of votes switched to third parties.

Accordingly, it will be shown below that major miscalculations or omissions can be made by ignoring vote migration or vote switching involving third parties. This is particularly true in seeking to determine definitively whether the Comey Letter was determinant in switching MWP to Trump. This book will highlight numerous pundits and observers who are either deniers or otherwise skeptical of any claims that there was any irregularity in the election. Because the issue being addressed is so critical, and in Davis' words, "of historical importance," we owe it to history to analyze the numbers with accuracy and as much precision as possible.

2.2. Modeling the Influence of Switching with Inclusion of Third-Party Candidates

The basic data listing the results of the 2016 presidential election and the margins needed for analysis is contained in Table 2-1 below.

Table 2-1 Key Vote Statistics From the 2016 Presidential Election States That Tilted the Electoral College to Trump Michigan, Wisconsin and Pennsylvania				
	Michigan	Wisconsin	Pennsylvania	United States Total
Clinton Votes	2,268,839	1,382,536	2,926,451	65,844,954
Trump Votes	2,279,543	1,405,284	2,970,733	62,979,879
All Third Parties	250,902	188,330	218,228	
Total Votes Vtot	4,799,284	2,976,150	6,115,412	
Trump Vote Margin by State MTR	10,704	22,748	44,282	
Trump % Margin by State =100*MTR/Vtot	0.22	0.76	0.72	
Electoral College Delegates	16	10	20	
Trump Total Margin in Michigan, Wisconsin and Pennsylvania = 77,734				
Clinton Total Margin in US = 2,865,075				
Data Taken from Wikipedia: Electoral College Votes: Trump 306, Clinton 232: Swing of the 46 MWP Delegates would Have Resulted in Clinton Winning the Electoral College and the Presidency with Clinton Having 278 Electoral Votes and Trump Having 260				

As a base of reference, the data by Silver and Davis for the Small Comey and Large Comey comparisons are listed in Table 2-2 below.

Table 2-2 Small Comey and Large Comey Comparisons to the Margins in MWP without Vote Doubling					
State	Trump % Margin MTRP	Small Comey Effect 1%	Large Comey Effect 4%	Small Comey Effect 1%	Large Comey Effect 4%
		Implied Percentage Margin For Clinton In the Absence of the Comey Letter: Per Silver and Davis		Implied Percentage Margin For Clinton In the Absence of the Comey Letter: With Doubling Effect z=0 (No Third Party Effects)	
	MTRP	1-MTRP	4-MTRP	2-MTRP	8-MTRP
Mich	0.22	0.78	3.78	1.78	7.78
Wisc	0.76	0.24	3.24	1.24	7.24
Penn	0.72	0.28	3.28	1.28	7.28

The analysis by Silver and Davis for Michigan as an example adds one and four percent to the negative number .22 and lists .78 and 3.78 as the effect of the Small Comey and Large Comey Effects. Similar calculations were done for Wisconsin and Pennsylvania. By observing that in the absence of third party effects, a loss of L votes by one candidate to the other dominant candidate leads to a difference of 2 L votes, one obtains the two right-hand columns in Table 2-2. For example, a Small Comey Effect of one percent for Michigan leads (with doubling) to a two percent difference and when the deficit of .22% is subtracted one obtains the quantity 1.78 shown in the Table 2-2 with similar results for the other two states and all three states using the 4% for the Large Comey Effect.

2-3. Computing the Tilt Margin with Third-Party Effects

The model parameters Tilt Margin, TM, Maximum Whammy Effect, MWE, and Maximum Whammy Effect Ratio MWER = MWE/TM are defined in Appendix I. The quantity z is defined as the fraction of votes in MWE that are switched to third parties with the remaining fraction (1-z) defined as the votes that are changed to the gaining dominant candidate. The value of the quantity MWER is that when it exceeds 1.0, the value of MWE has exceeded the Tilt Margin, TM, and the switching of votes was thus pivotal.

If z=0, (no third party), the Tilt Margin TM=MTR/2. This is so, as stated above, because if Clinton loses A votes that go to Trump (or vice versa), the resulting difference is 2A. If z=1, with all of the switched votes going to third parties TM=MTR. In this case, the other dominant candidate gains no votes, however since his/her opponent has lost votes to third parties, he/she has gained that number of votes difference (on the margin) but with no doubling. These two conditions occur inherently through the definition TM=MTR/ [2(1-z/2)] as derived in Appendix I.

Table 2-3 lists MWER as a function of z for a 1% Comey Effect. The results indicate that for all values of z, MWER exceeds 1.0, hence as mentioned earlier, a 1% Comey Effect, even with third party effects, leads to Clinton retaining a lead over Trump.

Table 2-3: Effect of Switching Votes Due to Comey Letter MWER Model Assumed 1% Effect for Full Range of z							
States	Vtot	Trump Margin MTR	Trump Margin %	MWER for 4 Values of z			
						z	
				0.0	0.5	0.75	1.0
Michigan	4,799,284	10,704	0.22	8.97	6.73	5.60	4.48
Wisconsin	2,976,150	22,748	0.76	2.62	1.96	1.64	1.31
Pennsylvania	6,115,412	44,282	0.72	2.76	2.07	1.73	1.38

Table 2-4 lists a calculation for the minimum percentage the Comey Letter effect needed to tilt the election to Trump in each of the three MWP states. With no third party effect, the minuscule level of .39% Comey Letter effect was enough to tilt all three MWP states. If all switched votes went to third parties ($z=1$) again, a minuscule percentage of .77 % was sufficient.

Table 2-4: Minimum Values of Comey Letter Percentage Effect, P to Tilt All Three MWP States (allowing for Full Range of Possible Third-Party Effects)						
States	Vtot	MTR	MWER for P=.39%, z=0	MWER for P=.52%, z=.5	MWER for P=.62 %, z=.75	MWER for P=.77%, z=1
Mich	4,799,284	10,704	3.46	3.46	3.46	3.46
Wisc	2,976,150	22,748	1.01	1.01	1.01	1.01
Penn	6,115,412	44,282	1.07	1.07	1.07	1.07

This book, along with numerous other analyses of the Comey Letter effect, has referred to polling shifts of 2.6% nationally, the Small and Big Comey analyses considered 1% and 4% effects. Additionally, polling results in the MWP states one week before the election[54,55,56] showed Clinton leads ranging from 4% to 7%. Table 2-5 was constructed to provide data for MWER to cover this full range of percentages (and values of z) as contrasted with the percentages needed in each MWP state to be pivotal.

Table 2-5 MWER for a Range of Values for P and z for the Three MWP States in the 2016 Presidential Election					
			Michigan	Wisconsin	Pennsylvania
		Vtot	4,799,284	2,976,150	6,115,412
		MTR	10,704	22,748	44,282
P %	z				
0.77	0		6.9	2.0	2.1
0.77	0.5		5.2	1.5	1.6
0.77	1.0		3.5	1.0	1.1
1	0		9.0	2.6	2.8
1	0.5		6.7	2.0	2.1
1	1.0		4.5	1.3	1.4
3	0		26.9	7.8	8.3
3	0.5		20.2	5.9	6.2
3	1		13.5	3.9	4.1
5	0		44.8	13.1	13.8
5	0.5		33.6	9.8	10.4
5	1		22.4	6.5	6.9
7	0		62.8	18.3	19.3
7	0.5		47.1	13.7	14.5
7	1		31.4	9.2	9.7

2-4. Comey Letter Effect on Late Deciders and the MWP Outcome

Blake[57] and Silver[52] provide data on late deciders, i.e., voters who made up their minds late, namely in the last few days before the election. Silver observed that "Voters who decided in the final week went strongly for Trump." Trump's edge amongst the late deciders in Wisconsin was 29%, 11% in Michigan, and 17% in both Pennsylvania and Florida. Given that the Comey Letter was such a national fixation by the press, TV, and the Trump election officials, it is natural to analyze how these late deciders (potentially influenced by the Comey Letter) might have tilted the election. The model for computing MWER for Late Deciders in Table 2-6 is derived in Appendix I, MWER ranging from 5.6 to 11.8 provides further evidence that the Comey Letter was pivotal in tilting the 2016 election to Donald Trump.

Table 2-6: Comey Letter Maximum Whammy Effect Ratio Caused by Late Deciding Voters							
State	Vtot	MTR	PC	PT	Percentage Undecided LD	TM	MWER
Mich	4,799,284	10,704	39	50	12	5,352	11.8
Wisc	2,976,150	22,748	30	59	12	11,374	9.1
Penn	6,115,412	44,282	37	54	12	22,141	5.6
MWER = Vtot * [(PT- PC)/100] * (LD/100)/[MTR/2]							

The conclusion drawn from this book's analysis is that the Comey Letter of October 28, 2016, given its maximum possible effect, allowing for only a fraction of the maximum possible effect—either by analyzing the poll results before the Comey Letter or by looking at the votes of late deciders—cost Clinton the election and led to Donald Trump becoming president. The data analysis using polling data just before the Comey Letter and late decider data both lead to the same conclusion: that only a small fraction of a Maximum Comey Effect was needed to tilt the three MWP states.

2-5. The Politics of Clinton's Email and Comey's Actions

Republicans, in December 2017, took a renewed issue with Comey and the FBI over their handling of the Clinton email controversy. This is most ironic in light of the revelation[58] that after the inauguration, six Trump White House staffers used private email for official White House business. This included Chief of Staff Reince Priebus, Chief Strategist Stephen Bannon, daughter Ivanka Trump, son-in-law Jared Kushner, and advisors Stephen Miller and Gary Cohn.

The use of private email by key White House staffers occurred despite the tightening of the applicable law in 2014 after Clinton left office and after the "lock her up" campaign.

During the campaign debates, Trump stated that Clinton would be investigated for her email misdeeds were he to be elected president. Trump's State Department did perform an after-the-election investigation of Clinton's alleged mishandling of classified information in her emails. The result of this investigation was completed in October 2019 and was summarized by Miller.[59]

> A multiyear State Department probe of emails that were sent to former secretary of state Hillary Clinton's private computer server concluded there was no systematic or deliberate mishandling of classified information by department employees, according to a report submitted to Congress this month.

The Comey factor was a one-time phenomenon and can be avoided in the future by the FBI and Justice Department adhering to rules that had been, and are, in place regarding disclosure of information related to on-going investigations. Voter suppression and fake news, however, pose a most continuing serious threat to the integrity of our election processes. This concern was further heightened in a report by Miller, Jaffe, and Rucker,[60] who observed that "Trump pursues Putin and leaves a Russian threat unchecked," the threat being the continued Russian meddling in US elections. Numerous pundits have opined that the "election is over, Trump won fair and square, and everyone should get over it."

Such positions, coupled with the Trump administration doing nothing about the Russian meddling and denying its role in the election, is contrary to the national interest. It is thus imperative to chronicle, in a contemporary manner—for history—the extraordinary forces that led to Trump becoming president and to remove the ambiguity of opinion on the effect of these forces that are described herein. While much has been written about all three factors, there is little detailed analysis on the mathematics of how Michigan, Wisconsin, and Pennsylvania were "tilted" to Trump because of the Triple Whammy. When all three factors (called whammies in this book) are examined, with detailed mathematical accounting, the implication of this book's becomes conclusive.

Chapter 3

The Second Whammy

3-1. Trump's Voter Fraud Commission and Operation Crosscheck

Given his severe disaffection for the role of the Electoral College as described by Abadi,[12] a logical early initiative for Trump would have been his forming a commission to study its role and its possible elimination in the presidential election process. Instead, Trump falsely bragged about his Electoral College win as "the biggest Electoral College win since Ronald Reagan," a false claim as reported by Dann.[61]

Instead of a commission to study the role of the anachronistic Electoral College,[62,63] which Trump so aggressively tweeted against four years earlier, he appointed a commission to investigate "voter fraud." Trump attributed his loss by 2.9 million popular votes as being due to three to five million fraudulent votes cast in the election—a claim disproved in detail by Blake,[64] who showed that "the math disagrees." Despite numerous studies that showed that the alleged voter fraud was a myth, Trump went ahead with the ill-fated commission and named Kris Kobach commission co-chair. Kobach,[65,66] as Kansas Republican secretary of state, had been "for the better part of a decade, the key architect behind many of the nation's anti-voter and anti-immigration policies."

As the commission proceeded, a Democratic member[67] sued the commission, claiming that he was being frozen out of the commission's activities. One of the critical initiatives Kobach and Trump sought to further institutionalize by the commission was "Operation Crosscheck," which Kobach had implemented before the 2016 presidential election in twenty-eight primarily-Republican states. Greg Palast, an award-winning investigative journalist, has reported extensively, and written a book describing both the intent and methodology of Operation Crosscheck.[9,10,68] This voter suppression tool, Operation Crosscheck, collected a massive database in the twenty-eight participating states on citizens who allegedly registered to vote in more than one state.

As Palast describes, the process is so flawed and so cleverly designed that it effectively disfranchises significant percentages of African Americans, Latinos, and those of Asian descent. Most interesting is the claim that multiple registrations are an indication of fraud rather than the fact that people who move from one state to another rarely choose (or remember) to cancel registration where they used to live. Ironically, five people in Trump's inner circle were found to be registered to vote in two states,[69] including:

- Steve Bannon, formerly Mr. Trump's chief strategist in Florida and New York;
- Tiffany Trump, Trump's youngest daughter in Pennsylvania and New York;
- Sean Spicer, former press secretary in Virginia and Rhode Island;
- Jared Kushner, Trump's son-in-law and close advisor in New York and New Jersey; and

- Steven Mnuchin, secretary of the treasury in New York and California.

Palast describes how the system is allegedly designed to work. "Crosscheck supposedly matches first, middle and last name plus birth date, and provides the last four digits of a social security number for additional verification."

However, in examining lists from several states, Palast found that:

> Crosscheck's results seemed, at best, deeply flawed. We found that one-fourth of the names on the list lacked a middle name match. The system can mistakenly identify fathers and sons as the same voter, ignoring the designations of Jr. and Sr. A whole lot of people named "James Brown" are suspected of voting or registering twice, 357 of them in Georgia alone. But according to Crosscheck, James Willie Brown is supposed to be the same voter as James Arthur Brown, James Clifford Brown is allegedly the same voter as James Lynn Brown ...

Palast refers to statistics that show that African American, Latino, and Asian names predominate in the Crosscheck matching process and that minorities are overrepresented in eighty-five of 100 of the most common last names. The names so selected are candidates for purging from the voter registration rolls. Some states send a post-card to each tagged individual (frequently with an old or wrong address), and if no response is received, their voter registration is removed. The outcome is discriminatory to minorities.

As noted by Wagner,[70] by January of 2018, many of the fifty states that had been solicited to provide voter data to Trump's Voter Fraud Commission, data similar to Operation Crosscheck, refused to give the data and Trump disbanded the commission, but only after tweeting, "the commission 'fought hard' to investigate allegations of voter 'abuses' because they know that many people are voting illegally, System is rigged, must go to the Voter I.D."

Typical of the sentiments opposing the commission, as quoted by Wagner, was that of former Missouri secretary of state, Jason Kander, who stated, "President Trump created this sham voting commission to substantiate a lie he told about voter fraud in the 2016 election … when he couldn't come up with any fake evidence, and under relentless pressure, he had no choice but to disband his un-American commission."

An excellent summary listing the twenty-seven participating states and the details of how Crosscheck works is an article by *Santa Cruz Indivisible*.[71] Michigan and Pennsylvania were two of the twenty-seven states using the Crosscheck system before the 2016 presidential election. Pennsylvania withdrew from Crosscheck in July 2017.

3-2. Voter Suppression Through ID Checks

It is well known and verified by several court decisions that voter suppression laws are a tactic that focuses on voter demographics for which a sizable majority vote for Democrats in states and/or sub-regions where voters provide a historic and sizable margin to Democrats. In addition to ID checks, voter suppression initiatives include reduction of early and Sunday voting, no same-day registration, disallowing student IDs without state driver's licenses for out-of-state college students, and failure to work toward shortening long waits for polling places with heavy leanings to Democrats. Voter suppression, both ID Checks and Operation Crosscheck, work as follows: Assume a district or state has a significant number of minorities, Latinos, elderly, disabled, poor, or college students for which statistics show the intended voter suppression law will deter or prevent a significant portion of these voters from voting.

Statistics and facts have shown that the type of ID frequently required has, for a sizable percentage of the targeted groups, been hard to acquire. Operation Crosscheck effectively works to cancel the registration of the same groups. Typically, such targeted groups of voters favor Democrats over Republicans by a range from 80/20 to 90/10 margin. In general, this can be characterized as follows: If the percentages in the historical voting pattern for the suppressed group is (D, R) where they vote D % for Democrats and R % for Republicans, the advantage to the suppression proponents (by suppressing the vote of the subgroup) is (D - R) %. If the state or district has a number, V, voters who do not vote because of the voter restriction tactic, the effective vote gained by the suppressor proponent group is V x (D - R)/100.

With Trump's small vote margin in the MWP states, this factor has great significance. It will be shown that voter suppression through an ID law was a significant factor in Trump's margin in Wisconsin, Michigan, and Pennsylvania (the three MWP states that tilted the Electoral College).

3-3. The Evidence for the Intent of Voter Suppression

Two contrasting articles characterize the lack of a consensus agreement regarding the role of voter suppression in the 2016 election. Lopez of *Vox*, in an article titled "Voter Suppression didn't cost Hillary Clinton the Election,"[72] concluded that voter suppression was not determinant in Trump carrying MWP or otherwise winning the election. On the other hand, a *Mother Jones* article[73] titled "Rigged: How Voter Suppression Threw Wisconsin to Trump—and possibly handed him the entire election" suggested the opposite.

Any discerning citizen who follows the broad spectrum of national news knows that there is a fierce national debate over the issue of voter registration laws that require photo type IDs. The opponents of these laws assert that this broad national effort has the objective of suppressing the vote of minorities, the elderly, disabled, and the poor who typically vote Democratic. There is no debate over the fact that this effort is heavily (almost exclusively) pursued by Republican legislators. Several studies have found that there is little to no significant incidence of voter fraud (the alleged rationale for these laws). Court decisions overthrew some of these efforts based on judges agreeing that the rationale of voter suppression was designed to favor the Republican party.

Wines[74] of the New York Times documents a statement made by Todd Albaugh, a staff aide to a Wisconsin state legislator, on Facebook, who quit his job in 2015 and left the Republican Party because of what he witnessed at a Republican caucus meeting. Allbaugh's statement on Facebook read:

I was in the closed Senate Republican caucus when the final round of multiple voter ID bills was being discussed. A handful of GOP Senators were giddy about the ramifications and literally singled out the prospects of suppressing minority and college voters. Think about that for a minute. Elected officials planning and happy to help deny a fellow American's constitutional right to vote in order to increase their own chances to hang onto power.

A second example from Wisconsin, listed by Wines, is, "In April of this year, Representative Glen Grotham, Republican of Wisconsin, predicted in a television interview that the state's voter ID law would weaken the Democratic presidential candidate Hillary Clinton's chances of winning the state in November's election."

Similar acknowledgments from Pennsylvania listed by Wines include the following, "In Pennsylvania, the state Republican Party chairman, Robert Gleason , told an interview that the state's voter ID law 'had helped a bit' in lowering President Obama's margin of victory over the Republican presidential nominee Mitt Romney in the state in 2012."

In that same election, the Republican leader of the Pennsylvania House of Representatives, Mike Turzai, predicted during the campaign that the voter ID law would "allow Governor Romney to win the state of Pennsylvania."

Pennsylvania's voter ID law, enacted in 2012, was struck down by court order in 2014.

3-4. Objectives and Methodology of the Mathematical Analysis

The thrust of this chapter is:

- Examine the parameters of voter suppression, including Operation Crosscheck and required IDs to include the maximum effect and the percentage of this maximum effect needed to switch each MWP state from Clinton to Trump;
- Examination of the totality of vote swings due to voter suppression against the "smallness" of the Trump margin in MWP; and
- Use of average estimate of the key variables represented in the mathematical model and parametric analysis.

3-5. The Mathematics of How Voter Suppression Through ID Checks Benefitted Trump in Wisconsin

In 2012, the Wisconsin legislature, under the Republican control of Governor Scott Walker, signed a law requiring voters to show a photo ID to vote. After lawsuits, US District Judge Lynn Adelman, in 2014, struck down the law, and his ruling determined that 300,000 registered Wisconsin voters lacked the type of ID needed to vote under the law.[75] The law, with changes, was reinstated before the 2016 election. On May 17, 2017, Senator Tammy Baldwin (D-WI) posted the following on Twitter, "Voter turnout in 2016 was reduced by approximately 200,000 votes because of WI's photo ID laws."

Lee, as described in *the Washington Post*,[76] gave Senator Baldwin's claim three Pinocchios, finding that the claim went too far. Using data and a methodology from the U. S. General Accounting Office (GAO), *the Post* suggested that the votes suppressed in Wisconsin were in the range of 61,000 to 94,000 in total.

In light of the various claims and counterclaims, a University of Wisconsin political science professor Kenneth Meyer conducted a polling survey, as described by Hasen[77] and Levine,[78] in Wisconsin's Milwaukee and Dane counties, and estimated that, in those two counties alone, 16,801 to 23,252 people were deterred from voting in the 2016 presidential election due to the Wisconsin photo ID law. Table 3-1 lists the Meyer estimate of suppressed votes in the two counties and GAO's assessment for the entire state.

The Wisconsin total population is four times larger than these two counties combined. Table 3-2 provides a projection of the effect of voter suppression in Wisconsin as a whole based on the Meyer analysis and a separate analysis by the US General Accounting Office (both extrapolated to the entire state). Tables 3-2 and 3-3 show how Trump's Wisconsin margin (the largest of the three in

MWP) was aided by the Wisconsin photo ID law and the resulting voter suppression.

3-6. Data on Voter Suppression in Wisconsin: 2016 Presidential Election

Table 3-1: Data on Voter Suppression in Wisconsin During the 2016 Presidential Election					
Data from Meyer Analysis: Milwaukee and Dane County Alone Data Source: Hasen[77]			Data from GAO Model for the Entire State of Wisconsin Data Source: Lee[76]		
Low Estimate	High Estimate	Average Between High and Low Estimate	Low Estimate	High Estimate	Average Between High and Low Estimate
16,801	23,252	20,026	61,000	94,000	77,500

Table 3-2: Extension of Meyer Analysis to the Whole of Wisconsin (Extrapolation Based on Minority Distribution in Wisconsin) Mayer Estimate for the Entire State of Wisconsin	
	Distribution of Wisconsin Minority Population
Milwaukee County	412,225
Dane County	99,253
Two County (Milwaukee and Dane) Minority Population Total VMD	511,478
Wisconsin State Total Minority Population	824,438
Wisconsin State Total Minority Population (Excluding Milwaukee and Dane) VOTH	312,960
Votes Suppressed in Milwaukee and Dane Counties VSMD (From Table 3-1)	20,026
# VSW = Total Minority voters suppressed in Wisconsin: Extrapolation from Meyer Analysis $VSW = VSMD[1 + VOTH/VMD]$	32,279
# Extrapolation of Minority Votes Suppressed to the Entire State of Wisconsin. $VSW = 20,026 [1 + 312,960/511,478] = 32,279$	

Table 3-3: Estimates of the Effect of Voter Suppression Through ID Checks on Trump's 2016 Margin in Wisconsin			
An Estimate of Votes Suppressed			
Vote Differences from 88/08 Split	Trump Election Margin in Wisconsin	Meyer Analysis Average Estimate Extrapolated for Entire State of Wisconsin	Whole of Wisconsin GAO Data Average Estimate
Number of Wisconsin Voters Not Voting Due to Photo ID Law Data Taken from Tables 3 and 4		32,279	77,500
Vote Differential Lost by Clinton Due to Voter ID Law in Wisconsin Based on .88 to 08% split Meyer (.88-.08) x .9 x 32,279= # GAO (.88-.08) x .9 x 77,500		23,240	55,800
Actual Trump Margin in Wisconsin	22,748		
Projected Trump or Clinton Wisconsin Margin had Voter ID Law Not been in Effect		492 Clinton Margin had there been no voter suppression MWER = 23,240/22,748 = 1.02	55,800 Clinton Margin had there been no voter suppression MWER = 55,800/22,748 = 2.5
# Factor of .9 used to reflect the likelihood of 10% of otherwise registered voters who might not have voted even had they not been suppressed/purged.			

After analyzing the voter data in Wisconsin margin with average estimates (Meyer and GAO) of votes lost due to voter suppression through the ID check, it is concluded that Trump carried Wisconsin as a result of the Wisconsin ID check process alone. When added to the effect of the Comey Letter, the evidence is overwhelming that these two whammies more than gave Trump his Wisconsin margin. As noted in Table 3-3, the Maximum Whammy Effect Ratio was 2.5 based on the GAO data and 1.02 based on the Meyer analysis.

On February 29, 2020, the *Wall Street Journal* reported[79] the following, "A Wisconsin appeals court on Friday (February 28) overturned a ruling that ordered the removal of up to 209,000 people from the state's voter rolls, handing Democrats a victory in a case they said was intended to make it more difficult for their voters to cast ballots in November."

3-7. The Mathematics of Operation Crosscheck

(Voter Suppression Effects on Michigan and Pennsylvania)
Table 3-4 contains data by Palast[10] from Operation Crosscheck files listing the number of voters' names pulled for screening, allegedly for suspicion of double voting because of being registered to vote in two states. Palast,[10] dated November 11, 2016, states:

> Trump signaled the use of "Crosscheck" when he claimed the election is "rigged" because people are voting many, many times ... His operative Kobach, who also advised Trump on building a wall on the southern border, devised a list of 7.2 million "potential" double voters—1.1 million of which were removed from the voter rolls by Tuesday.

Referenced in the quote was Election Day, November 8, 2016. The purge percentage was thus 15.3 %.

Table 3-4 shows that Operation Crosscheck alone effectively took over 49,000 votes away from Clinton in Michigan, which was almost five times larger (MWER of 4.6) than Trump's eventual margin of 10,704 votes. In Pennsylvania, Crosscheck alone took close to 38,000 votes from Clinton, which was 86% of Trump's Pennsylvania margin of 44,282 votes. For Pennsylvania, the MWER being less than 1.0 implies that voter suppression alone was insufficient to overturn Pennsylvania's electoral votes.

Table 3-4: Number of Voters' Names "Pulled" and Numbers Purged by Operation Crosscheck and Estimates of Clinton Votes Lost Adding to Trump's Margin.				
State	Trump's Margin by State MTR	Number Pulled by Crosscheck C	Estimate of 15.3 % Purged P= C x .153	Clinton Votes Lost (88%/8% Split)# P x [.88 - .08] x .9
Michigan	10,704	449,000	68,697	49,462 MWER = 4.6
Pennsylvania	44,282	344,000	52,632	37,895 MWER = .9
MWER = Px [.88 - .08] x .9 /MTR				

3-8. Conclusions Drawn from the Effect of the Comey Letter and Voter Suppression in the Three MWP States

- A small Comey Letter Effect alone switched all three MWP states from Clinton to Trump;
- Voter suppression alone switched Michigan and Wisconsin from Clinton to Trump; and
- A combination of a "very" small Comey Letter Effect and voter suppression switched Pennsylvania from Clinton to Trump. With voter suppression yielding an MWER of .9 in Pennsylvania, any combination from the Comey Letter and fake news exceeding 0.1 was sufficient to have kept Clinton as the winner.

Chapter 4

The Third Whammy

4-1. Author's Note Related to this Chapter

When I first wrote about this topic on my blog in 2017, I did so with some uncertainty and doubts. I was of the opinion then and now that any effort to apply mathematics to social and political phenomena is fraught with difficulty. Unlike physics and mathematics, there are no (or few) accepted theories or fields to which agreed-upon formulas can be attached.

As noted later in Appendix I, I overestimated one of the key parameters that are crucial to modeling the impact of fake news. I was fully aware of this possibility at the outset but proceeded to perform a best-effort, given what I did know, given the techniques and data available. Briefings by federal officials regarding Russian involvement in the election, plus related discussions on any potential effect on the election from fake news, have been met with most officials (when testifying or opining) including one of these caveats:

- There is no evidence that the Russians and/or fake news generally had any effect on election results; and

- No analysis or conclusion could be made concerning social media and/or the Russians having a pivotal or determinant impact on the election results.

I disagreed with the first statement above. Concerning the second statement, I had the following belief: It is difficult to put numbers to determine how voters are or were influenced by information and points of view. This is particularly true for data that is purposely false and whose falsity was designed to create a point of view that would lead the viewer/reader to favor or disfavor a candidate.

As a result, most pundits or officials who have no facility with mathematics or analytic analysis shy away from making a claim (other than generalities) that the factors cited have any effect on the election. This chapter is devoted to developing my best understanding of the effect of social media and Russian meddling and its impact on voting in Michigan, Wisconsin, and Pennsylvania (MWP) and the Electoral College outcome in the 2016 election.

In my experience in the scientific arena, a scientist or analyst delving into a new endeavor writes an early, perhaps first, paper on a topic and subjects it to peer review and publishes the paper in the general and open literature. Any aspect of the writer's claim, perhaps a new theory or finding, is thus free to be examined, critiqued, and possibly found to be partly or totally in error.

This is good because, in the end, such a paper advances the state of knowledge and works toward defining the degree to which there is a measure of agreement or certainty on the specified topic. And finally, one should note that if the scientist who wrote the first or early paper on the issue had shied away from doing so, for fear of criticism and possibly being wrong, then the subject of the topic would either remain obscure or too long be subject to conjecture.

These observations were recently furthered as I reworked Chapter 2 of this book to include the critique of the Nate Silver articles and Lanny Davis book on the Comey Letter Effect and the consideration of vote swings to third-party candidates. From that critique, one could conclude that a statistical analyst, as highly noted as Nate Silver, could have their methodology improved through other analysts suggesting improved methodology. In particular, I cite Silver's heretofore absence of accentuating the vote doubling feature and the influence of third parties in the modeling of the phenomena.

So my call to readers who may agree or disagree with the essence of this book's chapter is please have at it—critique my methodology and/or results with your best shot, but please do so with logic, analysis, and reasoning. Also, please document and provide your analysis in a web-accessible forum so that the collegiality (and state of understanding and acceptance) that I described above for the scientific process can occur and be furthered.

4-2. Assessment of the Russian Objective, Independent of its Effectiveness

The intelligence findings, an abstract of which is listed in Appendix II, which date back to January 2017, are compelling in their assertion of Russian efforts to assist Donald Trump's election as president. It is clear that the broad and extensive reach of social media and the internet was harnessed by the creation and circulation of fake news toward a corrupt end in the election of 2016 and is a considerable current and future threat to our democracy. It is also clear that the information grouped under the title fake news had two primary origins:

- domestically from within the United States; and
- Russian and some additional foreign sources.

The CEO and founder of Facebook, Mark Zuckerberg, initially denying that Facebook had any effect on the election result, as the major internet circulator of fake news, led to delaying the needed scrutiny merited by a topic of this national import.

4-3. The Public's Early Exposure to the Commercialization of Fake News

Shortly after the election of 2016, news circulated about a Macedonian teenager[80] and his entrepreneurial endeavor of harnessing what had come to be known as fake news. The teen described how he had made $60,000 by writing about issues and personalities involved in the election, which were fake (i.e., not true), but which by their description would resonate with some voters. The process described by the teen harnessed firms on the internet that effectively acted as hosts for disseminating posts and paid the developer by the click, meaning the number of times individuals accessed the posts on their site.

In the process, the individual reader was exposed to advertisements on the site, which completes and explains the commercialization of the process. The teen described how it was more profitable to focus on fake news posts that were pro-Trump and/or anti-Clinton. He told NBC News that at least 300 other locals had made a fortune in ad revenue[80] during the presidential election.

4-4. Trump Denies Any Effect of Russian Fake News

On May 30, 2019, *the New York Times* reported[81] that Trump posted the following on Twitter that morning, "I had nothing to do with Russia helping me to get elected." *The Times* then stated how, later in the day, Trump, at an impromptu press conference, seemed to correct this post by stating, "Russia did not help me get elected … I got me elected. Russia did not help me at all. Russia, if anything, I think, helped the other side."

At a press conference in Helsinki,[82] commenting on Russia's involvement in the US 2016 election, Trump was recorded on TV to state:

> I will tell you that President Putin was extremely strong and powerful in his denial today … have President Putin, he just said it's not Russia. I will say this. I don't see any reason why it should be.

Historians will debate and analyze this issue for decades, and scores of pundits and researchers have already done so. What is clear, however, is that Russia sought and was extremely active to help Trump get elected.

Several weeks after the election, on January 6, 2017, the Office of the Director of National Intelligence published a document[83] titled, "Assessing Russian Activities and Intentions in Recent US Elections—Intelligence Community Assessment." Excerpts include:

- The Russian campaign was multifaceted: Moscow's use of disclosures during the US election was unprecedented, but its influence campaign otherwise followed a Russian messaging strategy that blends covert intelligence operations—such as cyber activity—with overt efforts by Russian government agencies, state-funded media, third-party intermediaries, and paid social media users or "trolls."

- Russia used trolls as well as RT as part of the influence efforts to denigrate Secretary Clinton. This effort amplified stories on scandals about Secretary Clinton and the role of WikiLeaks in the election campaign.

Additional excerpts from this document are included in Appendix II of this book. Subsequently, two different studies were conducted for the Senate Subcommittee on Intelligence.[84,85] All three studies found significant evidence that there was an extensive effort by Russia to utilize social media such as Facebook, Instagram, Twitter, and others to tilt the election to Trump over Hillary Clinton. These studies did not include analysis of the degree of likely vote swings that ensued from the Russian effort. Similarly, the Mueller Report, while listing numerous instances of possible obstruction of justice, did not provide evidence of the Trump campaign colluding with Russia.

4-5. The Issue of Collusion with Russia and the Mueller Report

In the aftermath of the Mueller Report, given no overt finding of collusion between Trump officials and the Russians, there has been a concerted effort by the Trump administration to minimize any exposure of the findings of the report regarding obstruction of justice. As recently as May 20, 2020, the Supreme Court[86] blocked the release of heretofore unseen redacted portions of the Mueller Report, which the House of Representatives has sought related to charges of Trump and his supporters having obstructed justice—one of the two charges during Trump's impeachment.

Meanwhile, Trump has steadfastly referred to the results of the Mueller Report as a "total exoneration," despite the unfinished/blocked Congressional investigation on obstruction.

The Mueller investigation was thorough and broad and, as a result, turned up illegal activities by several US and scores of Russian operatives who have since been convicted. Altogether, the Mueller investigation led to the indictment of thirty-four individuals.[87]

There was a close association between Trump, his presidential campaign, and those charged and convicted (including Paul Manafort, Carter Page, Rick Gates, Michael Cohen, and Michael Flynn). The fact that charges did not specifically include collusion has been fodder for Trump, calling the whole Mueller investigation a hoax.

The Mueller Report and related investigations, as noted above, revealed that numerous senior advisors to Trump had Russian ties and involvements. The sheer number of these entanglements establishes the big lie of the concept that the investigation itself was, as Trump-declared, "a hoax."

Simply put, any situation of such great national import, with such underlying entanglements of key officials with an adversary such as Russia, would generally cause any discerning citizen to demand an official investigation. Seemingly, this was the rationale for the Mueller investigation. For example, Trump's campaign director, Paul Manafort, took the assignment pro bono with the widely held belief that he sought a relationship with Trump and the campaign as a means to pay his indebtedness to prior Ukrainian connections.

The Manafort connections included a deposed pro-Russian Ukrainian leader who fled in exile to Russia. Other close associates such as Carter Page and Rick Gates had extensive business relationships in Russia and, like Manafort, became integral components of Trump's advisory circles. Chapter 5 includes the description of General Michael Flynn's payment by the Russian firm RT and a photograph showing Flynn sitting next to Vladimir

Putin. In Appendix II, the Intelligence findings describe the role of the Russian firm RT as a propaganda arm of the Russian government. These and other individuals who were charged and convicted were indeed convicted for crimes other than collusion. Nevertheless, it will remain for historians to wade through the history, much of it redacted in the Mueller Report, as to whether the investigation itself was warranted.

This book does not delve further into whether there was collusion. Instead, the focus of this chapter is the effect of fake news and cyber warfare. There is no unresolved issue as to the reality of widespread fake news and/or the Russian participation in cyberwarfare during the 2016 presidential campaign. The issue is twofold:

- How many votes did fake news and cyberwarfare swing, and from and to which candidate?
- What platforms were used, and who (domestic, foreign, Russian) was behind the effort?

The term fake news seemed to have been inserted into our lexicon early during the presidential campaign of 2016 before Trump tried to preempt the meaning of fake news to describe press elements that wrote unfavorably about him. In January 2017, I posted a paper[88] titled, "Mathematics Shows that Fake News Elected Trump as President." The paper focused on the effect of fake news alone on election results in the three MWP swing states and how these three states, despite Clinton's national 2.9 million popular vote margin, tilted the Electoral College results to Donald Trump.

The assumption was made that fake news efforts were uniformly applied to voters in all states. Despite this assumption of no targeting, the paper concluded that fake news alone tilted more than 39,000 votes away from Clinton (with the doubling effect), yielding a Trump margin of 78,000 in MWP, resulting in these three states' Electoral College votes going to Trump. That paper was followed by a more detailed paper[89] titled, "Mathematics of a Triple Whammy: How the Combination of the Comey Letter, Voter Suppression, and Fake News Tilted Michigan, Wisconsin and Pennsylvania, and the Electoral College." This book is an update and extension of that paper.

4-6. The Research Findings Establish the Reality of the Russian Cyberwarfare Effort

Findings and key results on Russian involvement reported by three experienced experts on cyberwarfare, fake news, and the Russian effort to elect Donald Trump as president in the 2016 election are listed in Tables 4-1, 4-2, and 4-3. A common feature of their three books,[5,7,90]—*The Plot to Hack America; Messing with the Enemy: Surviving in a Social Media World of Hackers, Terrorists, Russians, and Fake News; and CYBER-WAR: How Russian Hackers and Trolls Helped Elect a President*—and many similar efforts, is that the analysis is generally qualitative and subjective, but stops short of definitive conclusions on whether the efforts tilted the election to Trump.

Unlike my intent, the three writers forego vote count predictions based on the calculation of votes switched away from Clinton to Trump. The three tables were extracted as a means to provide the reader with a general understanding of the depth and extent of the Russian effort to elect Donald Trump and serve as a prelude or quick background summary to understand the details, techniques, and extent of both domestic and Russian use of cyberwarfare for the intended effect.

Book Page*	Table 4-1: Extracted Quotes from *The Plot to Hack America* by Malcolm Nance[5]
x	The Russians were putting a digital thumb on the scale of the US election to help the ... reality TV host—who just happened to be running on the most pro-Russia platform in GOP history.
xi	Beginning in March and April 2016, an unknown person or persons hacked into the computer servers of the Democratic National Committee.
xiv	WikiLeaks ... activist Julian Assange leaked the stolen documents with the intent to damage Hillary Clinton
xiv	How did information from just one political party gets released to the benefit of the unpredictable Republican candidate?
61	The hackers selected damaging excerpts from the cache of stolen data and then leaked them at a pivotal moment in the presidential election.
120	The FSB would create a false flag source to feed Assange the data taken from the DNC and any subsequent hacks through Guccifer 2.0.
*Refers to pages in *The Plot to Hack America* by Malcolm Nance	

Book Page**	Table 4-2: Extracted Quotes from *Messing with the Enemy: Surviving in a Social Media World of Hackers, Terrorists, Russians, and Fake News* by Clint Watts[90]
160	A prime example of its (Russian) assistance is the strategic dumping of the stolen John Podesta emails less than an hour after Trump's disastrous sexist "grab 'em by the pussy" comments hit the airways.
161	Without the Russian effort, I believe Trump would not have even been within striking distance of Clinton on Election Day.
161	No one will ever be able to prove within a doubt whether Russia did or did not win the election for Donald Trump ... my hypothesis is that Putin won at least two states for Trump, Michigan, and Wisconsin.
175	Regardless of whether Trump won because of Russia or through his disruptive style and populist message, Russia achieved a major victory when Trump became president.
** Refers to pages in *Messing with the Enemy: Surviving in a Social Media World of Hackers, Terrorists, Russians, and Fake News* by Clint Watts	

Book Page***	Table 4-3: Extracted Quotes from *CYBER-WAR: How Russian Hackers and Trolls Helped Elect a President* by Kathleen Hall Jamieson[7]
xii	"He [Putin] said he didn't meddle—I asked him again...You can only ask so many times. I just asked him again. He said he absolutely did not meddle in our election. He did not do what they are saying he did"- President Trump, November 11, 2017.
xiii	Putin's response on July 16, 2018, Helsinki Press Conference on being asked (by Jeff Mason of Reuters) whether he wanted President Trump to win, "Yes, I did. Yes, I did."
14	The verdict is [likely to be rendered] not with certainty but with a preponderance of evidence.
29	March 2, 2018. Putin interview with NBC's Megyn Kelly, when asked about Russian hacking, Putin responded, "Well, all right, Russians, but they were not state officials. Well, Russians—so what?"
43	After Clinton's "deplorable" remark, the Russian troll named FanFan was changed to "Deplorable Lucy," gaining a network of followers up to 70,000, leading to unison between Russian trolls and US followers.
*** Refers to pages in *CYBER-WAR: How Russian Hackers and Trolls Helped Elect a President* by Kathleen Hall Jamieson	

The findings of the intelligence agencies summarized (see Appendix II) plus the extensive research by the three authors, as summarized in the tables above, leave little doubt that the Russians not only sought to assist the election of Donald Trump but engaged in a well-designed and aggressive campaign to do so. The nature and design of the Russian campaign, and a similar campaign by domestic actors, frequently overlapped and/or melded into a joint or complementary effort.

The nature of social media is that bad actors seeking to push a negative story on a candidate generally do so independent of the source. Thus, a Russian troll-initiated negative story on Clinton (or a pro-Trump story) would commonly be picked up by domestic actors, and the circulation would be energized on Facebook, Twitter, etc. So, the question for historians is and will be not whether the Russians were involved but whether they tilted the election to Trump. The purpose of this chapter is to advance the science of answering this latter question.

Past and current efforts at mathematical modeling of the effect of fake news require two key variables, namely fake news exposure rate and fake news persuasion rates—two variables with considerable uncertainty. These, in turn, make the task of predicting whether fake news was pivotal itself an uncertain endeavor. As stated earlier, it behooves the scientific community to make the best effort at modeling with the intent of developing a growing history of sophistication and improvement in the overall methodology. This book and, in particular this chapter, is devoted to that end.

This chapter revisits the effect of fake news alone (both domestic and Russian) with a more careful examination of the mathematics and the driving parameters of exposure rate and persuasion rate. An additional factor of uncertainty is that of distinguishing between domestic and Russian fake news. The approach taken herein is a technique referred to as "parametric analysis." In this type of analysis, one makes a best effort to represent the phenomena of interest with key variables to represent the critical driving components of the phenomena. Where there is uncertainty, the analyst then puts reasonable bounds on the key variables and parameters and then provides tables and graphs representing the phenomena for the full span of variation in the parameters and variables.

Two variables that are dominant in modeling the effect of fake news are the following:

- The exposure rate E is the number of times a voter is exposed to fake news during the contemplation time in a period before the election.

- The persuasion rate P is the probability fraction that exposure to fake news, favoring one candidate over the other, is sufficient to cause that voter to switch to the other candidate.

Both parameters are meant to be representative across the voting public. Additionally, each quantity E and P vary according to the candidate the purveyor of fake news is seeking to help or hurt. The inherent uncertainty in these two measures arises from a variety of factors. Such factors include:

a) How big is the lie, and is it plausible?
b) Is it easily fact-checked and/or disputed?
c) How far-reaching is it in effect on the average voter?

Regarding the exposure rate, the questions affecting uncertainty include:

a) How often has the same lie been read by the same reader, thereby inflating the statistics on exposure rate?
b) Is the reader a likely voter?
c) Is the reader influential in converting other voters?

One means to address the dilemma posed by these uncertainties is to perform a parametric analysis that shows a model prediction of vote swings for a wide range of exposure rate and persuasion rate and the effect of targeting MWP. It allows the reader to apportion this third whammy with the other two whammies to address the conclusion of this book's title that, as a result of these three whammies, Trump's presidency is illegitimate.

The model developed herein refers to and use of the work of the National Bureau of Economic Research's (NBER) Hunt Allcott of New York University and Matthew Gentzkow of Stanford University. The authors wrote two papers[91] titled "Social Media and Fake News in the 2016 Election." Their first paper was not peer-reviewed and was subsequently updated and replaced with two follow-up papers,[92, 93] each on the same topic.

Hereafter, their three papers will be referred to as AG1, AG2, and AG3, in the order of publication. Their work was the result of extensive polling and related research seeking to establish the exposure and persuasion rate of Trump and Clinton voters to fake news. Their methodology will be described and extended in Appendix I. They concluded that for fake news to have led to Trump carrying Michigan, Wisconsin, and Pennsylvania would require that the average fake news story would have to be as persuasive as thirty-six campaign commercials having an average persuasion rate of .02%.

Numerous articles in the press quickly reacted to this first AG1 paper with headlines trumpeting the conclusion (based on the paper) that fake news did not affect the Electoral College results. Gentzkow was later quoted by Crawford,[94] stating, "that conclusion depends on what readers think is a reasonable benchmark for the persuasiveness of an individual fake news story."

Shortly after the first, non-peer-reviewed paper was available on the internet, the authors published a revised document, AG2, which made an incidental comment on the calculation described above and seemingly downplayed the calculation by stating in their conclusion:

> In the aftermath of the 2016 presidential election, it was alleged that fake news might have been pivotal in the election of President Donald Trump. We do not provide an assessment of this claim one way or the other.

By contrast to this low level (.02% or .0002) persuasion rate based on TV political advertisements, Anderson,[95] seeking a related statistic on persuasion rate, found that 17% say that social media has helped to change their views on a specific political candidate with Democrats slightly more likely to do so. Craig Silverman[96] reporting on a study done by IPSOS for *BuzzFeed*, reported on respondents' beliefs related to five pro-Trump/anti-Hillary Clinton fake news stories. For these five fake news stories, between 64% and 84% of the respondents "recalled seeing the headlines and believed the subject articles to be very or somewhat accurate."

These findings suggest, for these fake news stories, a persuasion rate more substantial than the .02% of a routine campaign commercial, is more realistic. In that context, it is believed that the AG1 paper—despite being an excellent academic paper—because of the widespread acceptance of the implicit (or implied) conclusion and how it arose, led to disarming the press, the public, and our national and state government officials as to the real threat posed by fake news. Several news articles in the press proclaiming that the AG1 paper settled the issue, namely that fake news did not affect the election, supports this assessment. A typical example of these articles is that by Bershidsky,[97] whose *Bloomberg* article, citing the AG1 paper, proclaimed in its title, "The Numbers Are In: Fake News Didn't Work."

The Poynter Institute, on behalf of Facebook (and reposted by *Breitbart News Network*), also analyzed the issue[98] and determined that "it is worth considering the possibility that fake news stories did not significantly impact the presidential election after all."

None of the various articles that appeared, similar to that of Bershidsky[97] and Warren (of Poynter), commented on the apparent weakness in the AG1 implicit conclusion, i.e., that the conclusion was based on the comparison with the low-end estimate of persuasion rate of routine campaign TV commercials. It should be obvious to any discerning individual that fake news, such as the five stories listed below, described in the Ipsos Silverman Buzzfeed article[96], had much more impact on persuasion rates than routine campaign commercials:

- A fake story on Facebook attributed to the nonexistent Denver Guardian. which declared in all caps: "FBI AGENT SUSPECTED IN HILLARY EMAIL LEAKS FOUND DEAD IN APPARENT MURDER-SUICIDE."
- A fake story picked up by British tabloids, Fox News, Russian news agencies, and various right-leaning websites. Fox headlined its story, "Clinton aide says Foundation paid for Chelsea's wedding."
- A fake story stated the following, "News outlets around the world are reporting on the news that Pope Francis has made the unprecedented decision to endorse a US presidential candidate. His statement in support of Donald Trump was released from the Vatican this evening."
- A fake story published before the presidential election accused a restaurant, Comet Ping Pong, in Washington of being part of a child abuse ring led by Clinton and her campaign chairman, John Podesta.

4-7. The Mathematical Model for the Effect of Fake News

This model, shown in Appendix I, includes the major variables employed in mathematics by AG1 with a detailed derivation of the mathematical model structure that serves to understand better

the variability and uncertainty of the key model components. In using the model as a predictor, a range of values for exposure and persuasion rates are used based on recent studies analyzing the full extent of the breadth of the fake news phenomena. The final results are expressed in a parametric form where needed persuasion rates to switch Trump versus Clinton winners are examined.

4-8. Allcott and Gentzkow Estimate of Exposure and Persuasion Rate and the Comparison with Campaign Commercials

The literature describes exposure variously in terms of shares, page visits, reach, and visitations. Allcott and Gentzkow, in AG1 and AG2, conducted an online post-election survey of 1,200 voters and a database of 156 election-related stories, 115 pro-Trump (30 million shares) and 41pro-Clinton. (7.6 million shares). They then used a ratio of twenty-page visits per share (not referenced), yielding 760 million instances of a user "clicking-through" and reading a fake news story.

Assuming a voting-age population of 254 million, they came up with an exposure unit of nominally 3.0 per voter, which they adjusted to 1.04 due to the polling results and a placebo effect they encountered. In AG1, Allcott and Gentzkow then applied an adjustment factor for the slant ratio in the stories. They merged the Trump and Clinton components of the model, similar to what was done in Appendix I, yielding an equation similar to Equation (12) in Appendix I. Using a representative value for the final election margins for MTR/Vac in the three MWP states (Michigan, Wisconsin, and Pennsylvania) of .0051 they obtained the equation:

1) $.69 \times Ec \times Pc = MTR/Vac = .0051$

They then used an exposure rate of $Ec = 1.04$ from their research, using the low end (.02%) or .0002 of the range described earlier as the persuasion rate of TV campaign commercials. This resulted in replacing Pc in Equation (1) above by $n \times .0002$ yielding

2) $n = .0051/ (.69 \times .0002 \times 1.04) = 36$

From this, they concluded that, for fake news to have altered Trump's carrying MWP, then the average fake news story would have to be as persuasive as thirty-six TV campaign commercials. Most significantly, as noted above, this observation was referred to obliquely and was deemphasized in AG2, as observed earlier, with Allcott and Gentzkow stating in the paper's conclusion that they "provided no assessment of the claim one way or the other" that fake news tilted the election to Trump.

The AG1 database for their analysis consisted of fake news articles that were circulated three months before the 2016 election—primarily on Facebook. The authors of AG1 make no distinction or description of the Russian effort or component of their fake news database. As noted in the next section of this chapter, hearings and reports provided to the Senate have demonstrated the reality that the voting public was exposed to a concerted Russian effort that was similar to that which Allcott and Gentzkow found in their analysis. Also, it is not clear how the AG study included shares that arose from media other than Facebook, such as Twitter, Alphabet (Google), Instagram, and YouTube.

4-9. Data Related to Estimation of Exposure Was Slow in Coming

Timberg[99] of *the Washington Post* related how Facebook, before the Congressional investigation, said that ads paid for by Russian operatives had reached 10 million of its users. Congressional hearings later found that this number was increased to 126 million for Facebook alone, 150 million when Instagram was included, and then 288 million when Twitter was included. In light of this new data, Facebook creator and CEO Mark Zuckerberg apologized for his earlier statement, "I think it was a crazy idea to suggest that fake news on Facebook helped sway the election."

The Russian operation is reported to have been executed by 1,000 operatives of the Internet Research Agency (IRA) working on Facebook, Twitter, Reddit, Google, Instagram, and other social media. Facebook handed over 3,000 ads to the congressional investigators and indicated that "126 million of its users may have seen content produced and circulated by Russian operatives." Timberg reports on a study done by Jonathan Albright of the Columbia University Tow Center for Digital Journalism. Albright, to describe "organic reach," stated:

> To understand Russia's meddling in the US election, the frame should not be the reach of the 3,000 ads that Facebook handed over to Congress and that were bought by a single Russian Troll Farm called the Internet Research Agency. Instead, the frame should be the reach of all the activity of the Russian-controlled accounts—each "post," each "like," each "comment," and also all of the "ads."

The *Wall Street Journal*[100] reported that the Kremlin support for Donald Trump on social media began much earlier than previously known. The *Journal* analyzed 150,000 deleted tweets that Twitter had identified in a group of 2,752. The *Journal* stated:

> The Russian-backed Twitter accounts were so successful imitating Americans that they were frequently followed and retweeted by prominent people, including Trump campaign insiders and mainstream media, including General Michael Flynn and Fox commentator Sean Hannity.

O'Sullivan[101] and Segall have described how Twitter's information to the Senate related to activity on its platform has been slow in coming. The article states:

> In September, Senator Warner of Virginia said ... the company said it had found only 200 accounts on its platform linked to the troll army. By late October, Twitter had found 2,700 accounts it said were run by the Internet Research Agency.

4-10. The Russian Cyberwar Operation Through the Internet Research Agency (IRA)

The US Intelligence Agencies' Report[83] was explicit in describing the concerted efforts by Russia to help elect Donald Trump as president in 2016. Subsequently, two reports provided to the US Senate Select Committee on Intelligence (SSCI) gave extensive detail on the Russian effort. These reports to the Senate[84, 85] are a must-read for any serious individual seeking to understand the nature, scope, intent, and effectiveness of the Russian operation.

As the presidential election of 2020 approaches, it is most disconcerting that President Trump has continually denied the effectiveness of the Russian effort to elect him, has failed to orchestrate countermeasures to avoid a repeat of the Russian effort and continues to treat Putin as a benign, potential partner for reconciliation.

The findings of the Senate reports referenced above are of importance to this book chapter because much of the reporting covers the depth and breadth of the various segments directed at the US voting public—namely exposure rate. Exposure is defined as the probability that a likely voter engages in reading, and thereby subjects himself/herself to change his/her choice of a candidate based on the content of the fake news. The fake news could be a post on Facebook, Twitter, etc. or it could be an ad or video (e.g., on YouTube) domestic or foreign (in particular, Russian). The Russian Internet Research Agency (IRA) was very active in defining, creating, and posting ads that, in their content, had the objective of several things, including:

- Changing voters' opinion about Trump or Clinton through false negative messages;
- Focusing on an issue that stirred resentment in a subpopulation, e.g., Black Lives Matter, LGBTQIA issues, Defense of Marriage Act, NRA, the Second Amendment, and Muslims; and
- Voter suppression efforts that caused voters to stay away from the polls.

An itemization of twenty of these topics, as constructed by the IRA, was done in the Oxford University study[84] and was defined as "segments," meaning they were directed at a segment of voters who might be most influenced by the subject covered in the segment.

Literature on the topic is confusing because of the variability of the content, the difficulty in obtaining precise data, and the question of how to "bin" the data by characteristic. Investigators have found varying willingness on the various providers, e.g., Facebook, Twitter, Instagram, etc., to make the data available. Data and its interpretation for this chapter were obtained from AG2,[91, 92, 93] Silverman,[96] Karpf,[102] and the two reports done for the US Senate[84, 85]. In the process of cataloging the data as it pertains to specifying exposure rate, E, the following descriptors related to exposure were encountered: They included:

- **Accounts**: Formal accounts on the internet, generally paid to a provider.
- **Sites**: Locations (including blogs) that can be found by internet users.
- **Stories**: Articles themselves or brief descriptors pointing to online references, press articles, or TV coverage.
- **Segments**: The Oxford study for the Senate categorized topics such as Black Lives Matter etc. as "Segments," and twenty are listed on page twenty-three of their report.[84]
- **Ads**: Advertisements appearing/posted on the internet.
- **Impressions**: Defined by Howard et al. Oxford Study, as the number of placements on a user's screen for all twenty "segments." Note that the actual number of clicks is only one-tenth of the impressions across a twenty-segment database. A possible implication is that 90% of users seeing an impression were not interested in the information displayed through the impression and chose not to read beyond what popped up on their screen.

- **Frame**: Albright defines a frame as the reach of the activity to include the ads posted, the reader, and all likes and comments from all viewers. This would be particularly applicable to Facebook.
- **Shares**: Assumed to be the same as a frame.
- **Clicks and reads**: Included in the Albright definition of "frames."
- **Engagements**: Defined by New Knowledge (page 21) to include shares, comments, and reactions such as "likes." This should be the same as "frames."

4-11. New Knowledge Fake News Study for the US Senate

The first study was done for the US Senate (hereafter referred to as New Knowledge Study[85]) on this topic was titled, "The Tactics and Tropes of the Internet Research Agency," and was authored by Renee DiResta and seven co-authors. The review included expansive data from Facebook, Twitter, and Alphabet (Google), plus additional platforms. The data (from pages seven and thirty-two of the report) have been analyzed in Table 4-4 below, seeking to determine an estimate of exposure rate. Page thirty-two of the report lists 76.5 engagements for Facebook and 187.2 engagements for Instagram. Page seven of the report lists the total audience engagement on Twitter as 73 million. In interpreting the New Knowledge data based on Table 4-4, the estimated value for exposure rate was 1.15, with component estimates as noted for Facebook, Instagram, and Twitter.

Table 4-4: New Knowledge Report for the Senate; Data Listing Fake News Engagements from Page 7 and Page 32 Reference[85]		
Media	Engagements	Period Covered
Facebook	76.5 million Page 32	Jan 2015 to Aug 2017 [31 months total]
Instagram	187.3 million Page 32	Factor = 24/31 = .8 Adjusted by dropping 8 months data after 2016 election
Twitter	73 million Page 7	
Regrams	20 million Page 8	
Total	357 million	
No. of Voting Age 248 Million		
Estimate of Exposure Rate E = (357/248) x .8 = 1.15 [Partitioned below between Facebook, Instagram, Twitter and Regrams]		
Facebook E= .24, Regrams E= .06	Instagram E= .60	Twitter E= . 24

4-12. The Oxford University CPRP Study for the US Senate[84]

In January 2019, the British University of Oxford published a research study done by Philip Howard and four co-authors for the US Senate SSCI titled, "The IRA, Social Media, and Political Polarization in the United States, 2012-2018." Their analysis examined the activities of IRA accounts on Facebook, Instagram, Twitter, and YouTube and how these activities microtargeted US voters with particular messages. Some of their conclusions were as follows:

- Over 30 million users between 2015 and 2017 shared posts on the various platforms;

- The activities were focused on Facebook, Instagram, and YouTube;
- The Russian IRA activities were designed to polarize the US public, e.g., African Americans, Mexican Americans, Hispanics and to encourage right-wing voters; and
- Efforts continued after the Russian effort was caught and publicized in the US

The data from the Oxford report's Table 5, page 35 (for Facebook alone), is listed in Table 4-5 below. The results of exposure equal to 0.3 are similar to the estimate of 0.24 based on the New Knowledge analysis of Table 4-4 and equal to the 0.30 value when Regrams are included with Facebook.

Table 4-5: Oxford Study for Senate Top 20 Facebook Pages (Facebook Only) [Data from Table 5, page 35 of the Oxford Study]	
Likes	38.7 million
Shares	30.8 million
Reactions	5.4 million
Comments	3.4 million
Total	74.9
No. of Voting Age 248 Million	Exposure Rate = 74.9/248 = .30 Facebook Alone

Despite the expected large variability of the estimate for exposure rate, two studies referenced above (New Knowledge and AG1) produce a nominal exposure rate near 1.0 implying each person in the US of voting age was exposed to at least one fake news story. The reality is that the distribution is skewed so that a portion of the voting-age population sees no or few fake news stories and another portion see several or many stories. Additionally, two of the studies that provide data for Facebook alone (New Knowledge and Oxford) yield estimates near 0.30. Where it was clear, e.g., the data from New Knowledge, that some data was taken for shares, etc., after the election was over, the data was adjusted.

Recent history has shown the reluctance of social media executives to fully share with the American public the full extent of the reach and breadth of fake news circulation on their platforms. Additionally, the *Wall Street Journal* reported[103] on June 17, 2020, that "A group of Russia-based hackers used sophisticated new techniques to spread disinformation in the US and avoid detection by social media companies for years."

Jonathon Albright was able to obtain data for his analysis because the media had a bug in its software that allowed his access—a computer virus, which was later fixed, denying future analysts access. The historical lack of access to the data, in addition to this latest report by the *Wall Street Journal*, suggests that exposure rate to fake news may be more significant than the numbers suggested above. Additionally, there are obvious benefits and strategies of focusing exposure to so-called battleground states with an emphasis on states most vulnerable to switching Electoral College votes. Accordingly, effective exposure rates higher than the nominal value of 1.0 inferred herein are/were likely. Therefore, the parametric studies done late in this chapter will extend the range of Ec to 2.5.

4-13. Mea Culpa - My Previous Overestimates of Exposure Rate Based on Timberg's Description of Albright's Analysis

In my blog post paper on Fake News Triple Whammy,[88,89] I referred to Timberg's paper[99] describing Albright's analysis of the breadth of IRA's activities. Timberg described how Albright had estimated 340 million shares arising from six (of 470) accounts on Facebook alone. In my posted article, I observed that Karpf[102] published an article in *the Washington Post* observing that Albright's use of the social media analytics tool called CrowdTangle, for monitoring Facebook interactions, was prone to overstate numbers. Based on the Karpf warning, I chose to be conservative in extrapolating the numbers Timberg listed (from Albright). Rather than extrapolating the 340 million shares that Timberg referenced for six to 470 accounts, I limited the extrapolation to 5% and 10% of the full extrapolation to 470 accounts. In hindsight, a further interpretation of the Karpf warning should have suggested that even the data Albright obtained, for the six accounts, might be in error due to the problems Karpf had found with CrowdTangle.

The results of my error were that I estimated the exposure rate to be as high as a range of ten to twenty. It should be noted that Albright was one of the six authors of the New Knowledge Report (above) to the Senate and that my calculations above suggest that their data leads to an exposure rate of nominally 1.0. It should be noted that Lapowsky[104] credits Albright with "conducting some of the most consequential and prolific research" on the tech industry's problems with owning up to the reach of fake news to include the late apology and admission by Mark Zuckerberg, founder and CEO of Facebook, that fake news was more extensive than early reports suggested.

The next section examines how targeting was directed at MWP, which suggests the need to extend the range of Ec in the parametric study.

4-14. Increased Exposure Ec Likely in the Targeted MWP States

The analysis of the three studies that sought to determine the exposure rate suggests the overall exposure rate was nominally

1.0. However, extensive intelligence findings, including the Mueller Report, suggest that Russian efforts were guided by polling and campaign strategy leading to directing efforts to so-called "battleground" states, commonly referred to as "targeting." The evidence is strong that the MWP states were targeted and that for these three states, Ec was likely significantly higher than 1.0.

Paul Manafort, as noted elsewhere, had extensive ties to Ukrainian leader Victor Yanukovych who fled in exile to Russia after being deposed. Given his position as head of the Trump campaign, Manafort was in a position to steer campaign efforts to battleground states, including MWP. The Mueller Report provides evidence that Manafort did so through his longtime associate Konstantin Kilimnik. Olson[105] describes a passage from the Mueller Report:[106]

> Among them is this nugget on Paul Manafort, who was Trump's campaign manager and chief strategist describing polling and strategy during an August 2, 2016, conversation with his longtime business partner Konstantin Kilimnik. Prosecutors described Kilimnik as having ties to Russian intelligence. The report says that wasn't the only instance of Manafort sharing internal polling data, and that "the sharing continued for some period of time after their August meeting.

Olson describes several references to Pennsylvania in the Mueller Report, including detailed interference efforts and planning of political rallies in Pittsburgh and Philadelphia advertised as "Miners for Trump," rallies which apparently did not occur.

The actual passage in the Mueller Report[106] on page 140 describes the August 2, 2016, meeting:

Manafort briefed Kilimnik on the state of the Trump Campaign and Manafort's plan to win the election. The briefing encompassed the campaign's messaging and internal polling data. According to Gates, it also included discussion of "battleground" states, which Manafort identified as Michigan, Wisconsin, Pennsylvania, and Minnesota.

Raju and Byers[107] of CNN describe the targeting of Michigan and Wisconsin, again, likely the result of the Manafort-Kilimnik ties:

> Some of the Russian ads appeared highly sophisticated in their targeting of key demographic groups in areas of the states that turned out to be pivotal ... The focus on Michigan and Wisconsin also adds more evidence that the Russian group tied to the effort was employing a wide range of tactics.

Targeting has the expressed purpose of increasing the exposure rate in the targeted states. Accordingly, the parametric analysis that follows will be extended to a range of 2.5 to allow for increased exposure—the actual magnitude, which is as yet undetermined.

4-15. Maximum Whammy Effect (MWE) Representation of Fake News Effect

The variables used below are identical in meaning to definitions used in Chapters 2 and 3, as defined in Appendix I, except the whammy here is fake news rather than the Comey Letter or voter suppression.

- **MWE:** Maximum Whammy Effect is the estimate of the total votes switched from Clinton to Trump by virtue of fake news expressed by MWE = Vac Ec Pc. This formula is derived in Appendix I, MTR is Trump's margin in a particular MWP state. Vac is the number of Clinton's votes in a particular MWP state. Ec and Pc are the anti-Clinton- pro-Trump exposure and persuasion rates.
- **TM:** The Tilt Margin is represented by TM = MTR/ [2(1-z/2)], as defined in Appendix I. TM equals MTR/2 for no third-party effects and TM = MTR/[2(1-z/2] if a fraction z of switched votes go to third parties
- **MWER:** Maximum Whammy Effect Ratio = Maximum Whammy Effect, MWE, divided by the Tilt Margin TM.

3) MWER = MWE/TM = Vac Ec Pc / MTR/ [2(1-z/2)]

For generalizing of tabular results (with and without third parties), it is preferable to make the entry tables in Table 4-6 with the expression:

4) MWER* = MWER/(1-z/2) = 2 x Vac Ec Pc / MTR

The parametric presentation in Table 4-6 represents MWER* based on Equation (4) and is computed for a range of levels of Ec and Pc developed in this book. To retrieve a value for MWER from Table 4-6, for a particular scenario representing a fraction z of votes switched to third parties, the entries for MWER* should be multiplied by (1-z/2). The darkened areas of Table 4-6 correspond to values of Ec and Pc where the maximum whammy effect ratio MWER* exceeded 1.0, meaning that the fake news effect exceeded the tilt margin.

Table 4-6: Fake News Maximum Whammy Effect Ratio MWER* for MWP and Range of Exposure and Persuasion Rates. Darkened areas represent levels of EC and Pc for which Fake News Alone Tilted an MWP state to Trump. [This table is based on Equation (4)]					
		Michigan	**Wisconsin**	**Pennsylvania**
	Vac	2,268,839	1,382,536	2,926,451
	MTR	10,704	22,748	44,282
Pc	**Ec**	**MWER***	**MWER***	**MWER***
0.001	1.0	0.42	0.12	0.13
0.002	1.0	0.85	0.24	0.26
0.003	1.0	1.27	0.36	0.40
0.004	1.0	1.70	0.49	0.53
0.005	1.0	2.12	0.61	0.66
0.006	1.0	2.54	0.73	0.79
0.007	1.0	2.97	0.85	0.93
0.008	1.0	3.39	0.97	1.06
0.009	1.0	3.82	1.09	1.19
0.01	1.0	4.24	1.22	1.32
0.001	1.25	0.53	0.15	0.17
0.002	1.25	1.06	0.30	0.33
0.003	1.25	1.59	0.46	0.50
0.004	1.25	2.12	0.61	0.66
0.005	1.25	2.65	0.76	0.83
0.006	1.25	3.18	0.91	0.99
0.007	1.25	3.71	1.06	1.16
0.008	1.25	4.24	1.22	1.32
0.009	1.25	4.77	1.37	1.49
0.01	1.25	5.30	1.52	1.65

0.001	1.5	0.64	0.18	0.20
0.002	1.5	1.27	0.36	0.40
0.003	1.5	1.91	0.55	0.59
0.004	1.5	2.54	0.73	0.79
0.005	1.5	3.18	0.91	0.99
0.006	1.5	3.82	1.09	1.19
0.007	1.5	4.45	1.28	1.39
0.008	1.5	5.09	1.46	1.59
0.009	1.5	5.72	1.64	1.78
0.01	1.5	6.36	1.82	1.98
0.001	2.0	0.85	0.24	0.26
0.002	2.0	1.70	0.49	0.53
0.003	2.0	2.54	0.73	0.79
0.004	2.0	3.39	0.97	1.06
0.005	2.0	4.24	1.22	1.32
0.006	2.0	5.09	1.46	1.59
0.007	2.0	5.93	1.70	1.85
0.008	2.0	6.78	1.94	2.11
0.009	2.0	7.63	2.19	2.38
0.01	2.0	8.48	2.43	2.64
0.001	2.5	1.06	0.30	0.33
0.002	2.5	2.12	0.61	0.66
0.003	2.5	3.18	0.91	0.99
0.004	2.5	4.24	1.22	1.32
0.005	2.5	5.30	1.52	1.65
0.006	2.5	6.36	1.82	1.98
0.007	2.5	7.42	2.13	2.31

0.008	2.5	8.48	2.43	2.64
0.009	2.5	9.54	2.73	2.97
0.01	2.5	10.60	3.04	3.30

4-16. How Pivotal Was Fake News Alone?

Regarding whether fake news was pivotal, Gentzkow, one of the early, key researchers on this topic, was reported[91, 92, 93] to have stated, "that conclusion depends on what readers think is a reasonable benchmark for the persuasiveness of an individual fake news story." For the reasons stated earlier, this whammy is the most difficult to assess. The best one can do at this stage of research is to examine results such as Table 4-6 and extract minimum values of Ec and Pc where MWER exceeds 1.0, i.e., namely the minimum, values of Ec and PC where the fake news effect MWE exceeded the Tilt Margin TM. In seeking to draw conclusions from these results, another level of uncertainty that arises is that of the exposure rate Pc. For example, the studies reported to the Senate, as discussed in this chapter, imply an exposure rate of nominally 1.0. If targeting is added, the exposure rate is expected to be larger than 1.0.

With these considerations, alternative presentations of Equation (3) are done in Table 4-7 and 4-8. The equation is solved separately for Pc (Table 4-7) and then for Ec (Table 4-8). In each instance, for both tables, a value of MWER =1 is used. The table results then provide an extensive listing of values of Pc and Ec for which the tilt margin TM =1. Additionally, by examining the structure of Equation (3), it is seen that the results can be extended for all values of MWER by simply multiplying the table results by the desired value of MWER.

Table 4-7 Values for Persuasion Rate Pc vs. Ec for MWP with MWER=1.0					
State	Ec				
z		0	0.25	0.5	1
Michigan	0.5	0.0047	0.0054	0.0063	0.0094
Wisconsin	0.5	0.0165	0.0188	0.0219	0.0329
Pennsylvania	0.5	0.0151	0.0173	0.0202	0.0303
Michigan	1	0.0024	0.0027	0.0031	0.0047
Wisconsin	1	0.0082	0.0094	0.0110	0.0165
Pennsylvania	1	0.0076	0.0086	0.0101	0.0151
Michigan	1.5	0.0016	0.0018	0.0021	0.0031
Wisconsin	1.5	0.0055	0.0063	0.0073	0.0110
Pennsylvania	1.5	0.0050	0.0058	0.0067	0.0101
Michigan	2	0.0012	0.0013	0.0016	0.0024
Wisconsin	2	0.0041	0.0047	0.0055	0.0082
Pennsylvania	2	0.0038	0.0043	0.0050	0.0076
Michigan	2.5	0.0009	0.0011	0.0013	0.0019
Wisconsin	2.5	0.0033	0.0038	0.0044	0.0066
Pennsylvania	2.5	0.0030	0.0035	0.0040	0.0061
$Pc=.5 \times MTR \times MWER / [Vac \times Ec \times (1-z/2)]$ Note MWER =1 for this Table and MTR for MWP are listed in Table 4-6					

Table 4-8 Values for Exposure Rate Ec vs. Pc for MWP with MWER=1.0					
State	Pc				
z		0	0.25	0.5	1
Michigan	0.001	2.4	2.7	3.1	4.7
Wisconsin	0.001	8.2	9.4	11.0	16.5
Pennsylvania	0.001	7.6	8.6	10.1	15.1
Michigan	0.002	1.2	1.3	1.6	2.4
Wisconsin	0.002	4.1	4.7	5.5	8.2
Pennsylvania	0.002	3.8	4.3	5.0	7.6
Michigan	0.005	0.5	0.5	0.6	0.9
Wisconsin	0.005	1.6	1.9	2.2	3.3
Pennsylvania	0.005	1.5	1.7	2.0	3.0
Michigan	0.01	0.2	0.3	0.3	0.5
Wisconsin	0.01	0.8	0.9	1.1	1.6
Pennsylvania	0.01	0.8	0.9	1.0	1.5
Michigan	0.02	0.1	0.1	0.2	0.2
Wisconsin	0.02	0.4	0.5	0.5	0.8
Pennsylvania	0.02	0.4	0.4	0.5	0.8
Ec=.5 x MTRx MWER / [Vac x Pc x(1-z/2)] Note MWER =1 for this Table Vac and MTR for MWP are listed in Table 4-6					

Figures 4-1, 4-2, and 4-3 provide an alternate parametric representation of the required values of Ec and Pc that lead to the third maximum whammy effect ratio MWER* exceeding the Tilt Margin. Here, as in Table 4-6, we have chosen to represent the parameter MWER* (from Equation (4)) to make the graphs independent of any assumed value for third party vote switching. Figures 4-1, 4-2, and 4-3 provide a parametric graphical analysis showing how this range of Ec provides needed persuasion rates Pc (for all three states) (compared to) the range of rates for ordinary campaign TV commercials (0.0002 to 0.01 suggested by AK1).

Given the nature of the falsehoods described in the numerous fake stories that were circulated by Russian trolls and others during the 2016 presidential campaign, reason suggests that typical fake stories were more effective than routine campaign TV commercials.

Figure 4-1: Required Persuasion Rate as a function of Exposure Rate for Switching .5, 1, and 1.5 Multiples of Trump's Michigan Margin of 10,704 Votes

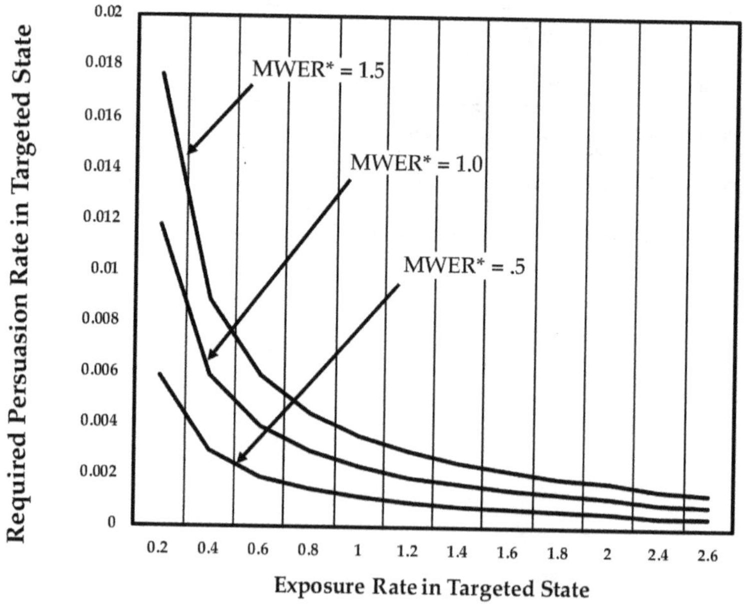

Figure 4-2: Required Persuasion Rate as a function of
Exposure Rate for Switching .5, 1, and 1.5 Multiples
of Trump's Wisconsin Margin of 22,748 Votes

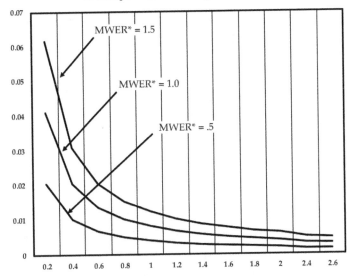

Required Persuasion Rate in Targeted State (y-axis)

Exposure Rate in Targeted State (x-axis)

Figure 4-3: Required Persuasion Rate as a function of
Exposure Rate for Switching .5, 1, and 1.5 Multiples
of Trump's Pennsylvania Margin of 44,282 Votes

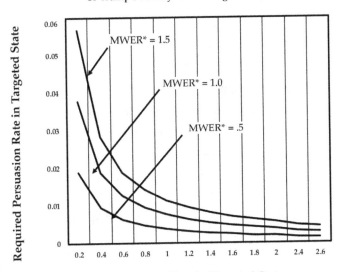

Required Persuasion Rate in Targeted State (y-axis)

Exposure Rate in Targeted State (x-axis)

Conclusions:

- **Comey Letter:** In Chapter 2, the conclusion was that the Comey Letter alone had the effect of causing the Electoral College votes of all three MWP states (Michigan, Wisconsin, and Pennsylvania) to switch from Clinton to Trump.
- **Voter Suppression:** In Chapter 3, the conclusion was that Republican-driven voter suppression alone had the effect of causing the Electoral College votes of Michigan and Wisconsin to go to Trump. In Pennsylvania, voter suppression was calculated to have affected 90% of the tilt margin so that only a 10% effect of fake news on Pennsylvania was needed for these two whammies, acting in tandem, to cause Pennsylvania's Electoral College votes to go to Trump.
- **Fake News:** As shown in this chapter, fake news/ Russian meddling have an effect that rises to the level of a significant fraction of the Tilt Margin, TM, and perhaps even more significant than TM. For example, it was shown in Chapter 2, Table 2-4 that in 2016 the Tilt Margins for the three MWP states were as small as .4% (for no third-parties) and .8% a full third party effect ($z=1$). The fragility of our elections, made possible by such small margins in key states, makes it so critical that elected officials must act to counter both sources— namely domestic fake news/Russian meddling.

Of the three whammies, this is the most difficult to characterize due to the following reasons:

1) Exposure rate is poorly quantified for several reasons, one reason being that some individuals have huge exposure and others very little—yet the parameter is essentially an average over the voting public.

2) Persuasion rate is also poorly quantified because fake news stories entail such a broad spectrum of falsehood and are targeted to special groups. Still, here, too, the parameter is an average over the voting public.

3) Mention was made in this book that Russian trolls initiated fake news and launched it in social media, and after that, it gets propagated by domestic sources. For example, the press has reported how Michael Flynn and Sean Hannity retweeted a fake news story of Russian origin.

Accordingly, assigning a measure to the separate effectiveness of Russian versus national fake news is, at most, difficult. Regarding whether Russian fake news was pivotal in tilting the Electoral College, the quote by Jamieson quoted in Table 4-3 seems most appropriate, "The verdict is likely to be rendered not with certainty but with a preponderance of evidence."

Clint Watts, in his book,[90] quoted in Table 4-2, stated, "No one will ever be able to prove within a doubt whether Russia did or did not win the election for Donald Trump ... my hypothesis is that Putin won at least two states for Trump, Michigan, and Wisconsin."

My hope is that this book and this chapter help to advance the state of understanding of this very critical phenomenon.

Chapter 5

Trump's Anti-Obama Syndrome

The nation (and the world) first observed Trump's anti-Obama syndrome when Trump claimed that Obama was born in Kenya and, therefore, was ineligible to be president. Few public figures could survive such monstrous untruths and elaborate sideshows—and be elected president. But such is the Trump phenomenon.

Perhaps Trump's continuing anti-Obama crusade can be explained by the happenings at the 2011 White House press dinner as described by Cohen:[108]

> Multiple news outlets have suggested that President Obama's mocking of Donald Trump at the 2011 White House Correspondents' Dinner provoked him to run for office. Trump tells a different story. Regardless, President Trump has declined to go to this year's dinner.

Pundits have since suggested that several of Trump's major initiatives arose from an anti-Obama syndrome. Observations support this claim in that several of Trump's initiatives—many openly admitted to by Trump—were an attempt to counter or reverse Obama initiatives. Many have brought extensive outcries. Examples include:

- Obamacare
- The Iran Nuclear agreement
- The Paris Climate agreement
- Regulations on the environment, food and product safety, and energy conservation

Trump's seeming obsession with Obama includes blaming the Obama administration for measures that Trump claims he had to take to fix or overcome as a legacy of actions or inactions by Obama. This became particularly true during the onset of the coronavirus pandemic, as will be described in Chapter 7.

5-1. Trump's Latest Obama Obsession: "Obamagate"

In May 2020, Attorney General William Barr announced that the Justice Department had recommended that the then-recent conviction of former Trump director of National Intelligence, Michael Flynn, be overturned. This action was quickly followed by Trump's launching of "Obamagate" as reported by Glasser[109] of *The New Yorker*. Flynn, a retired three-star lieutenant general, first came to national attention as a Trump national security advisor during the 2016 campaign, with his "lock her up" pronouncement, referring to Hillary Clinton and the email issue. The general had a storied career but fell out of favor late during the Obama administration.

During the transition of power, Obama advised Trump not to include Flynn in the Trump administration. After retirement, Flynn had engaged in unregistered lobbying on behalf of Turkey, and a photo emerged of his sitting next to Putin at a controversial meeting in Russia, for which RT, a Russian-funded TV station, paid him $45,000. The intelligence findings (extracts listed in Appendix II) of the Russian meddling in the 2016 presidential election described the role of RT as follows:

> Russia used trolls as well as RT as part of the influence efforts to denigrate Secretary Clinton. This effort amplified stories on scandals about Secretary Clinton and the role of WikiLeaks in the election campaign.

Ignoring Obama's advice that Flynn was bad news, Trump named Flynn to be his first national security advisor.

During the 2016 campaign, US intelligence agencies (as described in Appendix II) had found extensive proof of how the Russians were meddling in the election, seeking to aid Trump's campaign. Additionally, during the campaign, it became widely known that the Russians had hacked the computers and email of the Clinton campaign. As widely reported and seen by national TV audiences during the campaign, related to news of this hacking, Trump, in front of the nation, urged further hacking by uttering the following words, "Russia, if you're listening, I hope you're able to find the 30,000 emails that are missing. I think you will probably be rewarded mightily by our press."

Before the election, as a result of the intelligence findings of Russian meddling, Obama sought to engage Senate Majority Leader Mitch McConnell to participate in a joint bipartisan effort to notify the two campaigns, and the nation, of the Russian efforts. Obama's objective in including McConnell was that of avoiding the action being thought of as being partisan to favor Hillary Clinton. McConnell refused. Conservative columnist Jennifer Rubin[110] quotes Vice President Biden's explanation of McConnell's stance on the issue, "Senate Majority Leader Mitch

McConnell stopped the Obama administration from speaking out about Russian interference in the 2016 campaign by refusing to sign on to a bipartisan statement of condemnation." Obama then set in place sanctions against Russian interests in retaliation for the election meddling.

Before the inauguration, Trump tapped Flynn as his projected director of national security. Flynn, in the interim, after the election, but before the inauguration, had two clandestine phone calls with Russian Ambassador Sergey Kislyak. Kiely[111] lists Flynn's timeline of involvement on his Russian calls when he reportedly urged Kislyak (hence Putin) to moderate or reduce the response to Obama's sanctions in anticipation/promise of similar moderation (regarding sanctions) by the incoming Trump administration. After the inauguration, the issue of Flynn's meeting with Kislyak, having been exposed, became a contentious issue in that such meetings by private citizens violate the Logan Act. Flynn allegedly denied having met with Kislyak, supposedly denied the same to Vice President Pence, and was fired by Trump for the alleged lie. Flynn was eventually convicted of a similar lie to the FBI, in addition to filing false papers related to his lobbying for Turkey. In May of 2020, Attorney General Barr, through an appointed prosecutor not involved in Flynn's prosecution, recommended vacating the conviction.

This action brought much condemnation as attested to by a letter, signed by close to 2,000 former Justice Department officials from past Republican and Democratic administrations, condemning Barr's action as a political favor for a friend of President Trump.[112] The rationale that Barr used, quickly trumpeted by Trump, was alleged wrongdoing by the Obama administration to include the FBI and various intelligence operatives. The claim arose that there had been a conspiracy against Michael Flynn—a so-called "unmasking."

The initial press accounts that rehashed the history of Flynn's phone calls with Kislyak centered on the observation that US intelligence agencies typically record similar calls. In such instances, the foreigner's name is explicitly listed in the documentation of the calls. The US individual in the conversation is sometimes registered by code—hence not expressly named. Depending on the importance of the intercept, key officials in the government would be informed of the identity of the US individual in the intercepted conversation who was listed by code. This practice is referred to as unmasking and is a routine, legal process as described by Reichmann,[113] to assure that high-level US interests that may have been compromised come to the attention of appropriate US officials.

As the news of Flynn's alleged unmasking became front and center, Trump quickly wove his latest anti-Obama fantasy. Glasser[109] of *The New Yorker*, explained Trump's launching of "Obamagate" as follows:

> Trump will not shut up about Barack Obama—not now, not ever. On Thursday morning, amid the gravest economic crisis in a century and a deadly pandemic that will have killed more than a hundred thousand Americans by the end of this month, Trump yet again accused his predecessor of culpability in "the biggest political crime and scandal in the history of the USA." Obama, he said, should be hauled before the Senate to testify. "He knew EVERYTHING," Trump added in his tweet, one of dozens of attacks in the past few days in which he has targeted "Obamagate." What crime, exactly, was Trump accusing Obama of? What should he testify about? Trump never said, and it's a safe bet that he never will.

At a White House lawn press conference, Trump, having made a similar charge, was asked by Phil Rucker of the *Washington Post*,

"What crime, exactly, are you accusing President Obama of committing?"

"Obamagate," Trump replied. "It's been going on for a long time," Trump added without offering specifics.

"What is the crime, exactly, that you're accusing him of?" Rucker asked again.

"You know what the crime is," Trump answered. "The crime is very obvious to everybody."

Trump amplified his interpretation of the crime in an interview with Fox Business Network,[114] where it was tied to former Obama officials, including former Vice President Joe Biden and FBI Director James Comey. They were alleged to have requested that Flynn be unmasked. Fox, reporting on the interview, tied "Obamagate" to the unmasking in the title of the article and recorded Trump as saying:

> It was the greatest political crime in the history of our country. If I were a Democrat instead of a Republican, I think everybody would have been in jail a long time ago, and I'm talking with 50-year sentences. It is a disgrace what's happened. This is the greatest political scam, hoax in the history of our country.

For perspective on the "Obama crime" of unmasking, Savage[115] reported in 2017, the first year of Trump's presidency, and reported before the current alleged Obama conspiracy, that there were 16,721 unmaskings, a significant rise from the year earlier. The "Obamagate" unmaskings were in a list provided by the Justice Department covering the time after the 2016 election and through January 31, 2017.

As the days ensued, "Obamagate" morphed as follows. Trump expanded the alleged crime beyond Flynn's alleged unmasking to blaming Obama and others for the "hoax" of the Russia investigation plus the Flynn unmasking. It turned out that the Flynn conversations with Kislyak were recorded by the FBI rather than the CIA, and there was "no" masking of Flynn's name after all. In other words, Flynn's name was explicitly listed in the FBI documentation. But never mind, by now, "Obamagate" had expanded to unmasking in general plus the crime of initiating the Russian investigation.

But the conspiracy turned out to be a bit much even for Attorney General Willian Barr. Forgey and Gerstein of *Politico* described Barr's reaction as follows,[116] "Attorney General William Barr on Monday issued an apparent rebuke of President Donald Trump's efforts in recent weeks to hatch various accusations of misconduct by former Obama administration officials." Barr was quoted as saying:

> The legal tactic has been to gin up allegations of criminality by one's political opponent based on the flimsiest of legal theories. This is not a good development. This is not good for our political life, and it's not good for the criminal justice system. As long as I'm attorney general, the criminal justice system will not be used for partisan political ends, and this is especially true for the upcoming elections in November.

Trump responded to Barr,[117] "I have no doubt that they [Obama and Biden] were involved in this hoax I think it's just a continuation of a double standard."

Meanwhile, judge Emmet Sullivan, who had presided over Flynn's case and sentencing, used a provision in court procedure to have retired Judge John Gleeson review the actions of Attorney General Barr in vacating Flynn's conviction. Gerstein and Chaney of *Politico* described Gleason's decision,[118] "The judge ... skewered Attorney General Barr's handling of the case describing it as an 'irregular' effort that courts would 'scoff' at were the subject anyone other than an ally of Trump ... these claims are not credible ... 'Indeed, they are preposterous.'"

Birtherism and "Obamagate" will remain thus far as two of Trump's most mendacious attempts to bash his predecessor, Barack Obama. Fox commentator (and in-house liberal) Juan Williams[119] has described a litany of anti-Obama comments made by Trump to include:

- Lack of investigation of Obama book deal;
- Crimea was taken away by Russia because Putin "outsmarted" Obama;
- Obama used wiretaps to spy on the 2016 Trump campaign;
- Obama was about to start a war with North Korea;
- Obama was turned down for a meeting with North Korea's Kim Jong Un;
- Obama made a policy to separate children from their parents at the border;
- He pulled out of the Transpacific Partnership (PPP) because Obama made a bad deal for the US; and
- Problems with the White House air conditioning.

With Barr becoming attorney general, and effectively becoming Trump's Roy Cohn, it seemed certain that, had Obama surveilled (or wiretapped) Trump's campaign, proof would have been found. No such evidence has ever been offered. Williams goes on to describe the many well-known and verified Trump peccadilloes and, in effect, asks, "What would Republicans say were these peccadilloes (a list was included) attributed to Obama?" The coronavirus provided Trump another opportunity to blame Obama for some aspect of the nation's ills.

From the beginning, it was clear that the overall Republican effort to overturn Obamacare (later joined in by Trump) was based not on principle but rather as a component of the overall anti-Obama syndrome. This was evident in the meeting described by Stein[120] in an excerpt from a book by Draper, which explained how, during the inauguration night period, fifteen key Republican congressmen and ex-Republican House Speaker Newt Gingrich met and "plotted out ways not just to win back political power, but also put the brakes on Obama's legislative platform."

Mitch McConnell, while not at the meeting mentioned above, similarly had described a grand plan[121] to stop Obama's legislative efforts by attaching riders to spending bills that would limit Obama policies on everything from the environment to health care, forcing Obama to accept the changes or veto the legislation and risk a government shut-down. In a similar comment, McConnell stated, "The single most important thing we want to achieve is for President Obama to be a one-term president."

Trump and the Republican's effort to overturn Obamacare eventually focused on opposition to the "individual mandate," the component of Obamacare that required everyone to have insurance, with a penalty applied to those who chose not to get insured. Ironically, the individual mandate was a creation of the conservative Heritage Foundation, which led to Republicans having to contort their logic in using this component in their ensuing opposition in creating a Kill Obamacare (KOC) Coalition.

The role of Stuart Butler of the Heritage Foundation in giving birth to the individual mandate is described in detail in a blog post written by the author in 2013. It is listed in its entirety in Appendix III of this book. As of this writing, lower court decisions have indicated the individual mandate is unconstitutional, and the Congress has amended the ACA to remove that provision. Trump and the Republicans are pressing the matter further with a case in court, urging the court to make the entirety of the ACA unconstitutional.

Meanwhile, Trump has continually stated that he and the Republican Party will replace Obamacare with "a phenomenal new health care plan."[122] No details have ever been shared with the American public on the nature of this plan. Most ironically, Trump's Attorney General William Barr is reported[123] on May 5, 2020, to have "made a push to persuade the administration to modify its position in the Obamacare dispute that will be heard at the Supreme Court this fall, arguing that the administration should pull back from the insistence that the entire law be struck down."

5-2. Trump's Abrogation of the Iranian Nuclear Agreement

Trump's ignorance of history is similar to his ignorance of science. His antics exemplified this during the Tank (a secure vault in the Pentagon) meeting described in Chapter 7 and Conway's listing of Trump's gaffes on both geography and history. His abrogation of the Iran Nuclear Agreement, signed by the US, United Kingdom, Russia, Germany, France, China, the European Union, and Iran is a case-in-point of significant consequence. In 2015, the nations described above, after months of negotiation, reached an agreement with Iran that specified details that limited Iran concerning the nature of and quantity of nuclear fuel that Iran was allowed to acquire and generate.

During the campaign of 2016, Trump described the treaty as "stupid" and vowed that if he were elected the treaty would be voided or vacated by the US As the rationale for the Tank meeting suggested, as described herein, Trump was ignorant of the history of Iran-US relations as described below; otherwise, why would any presidential candidate make—and eventually act on—such a major international joint agreement with no rational argument to counter the wisdom of the world's great nation signatories.

Anyone living during the Cold War with the Soviet Union should appreciate the value of time and cool headedness in the cooling of antagonism between countries. For example, the Berlin Air Lift and later the "tear down" of the Berlin Wall eventually led to the unification of East and West Germany. Similarly, the US-Japan relations have become harmonious despite the antagonisms of Pearl Harbor and the US atomic bombing of Nagasaki and Hiroshima.

The Trump coziness with Vladimir Putin, while controversial in its details, nevertheless has facets of a similar nature. Trump's approach to North Korea's Kim Jung-un could be given similar credence were it not marked by the sheer monstrosity of the North Korean leader's regime such as:

- The alleged killing of his uncle with an antiaircraft gun while numerous relatives and others were forced to watch the murder; and
- The thousands of North Korean citizens in confined, forced labor camps.

The question thus arises as to what has caused the US and Iran to be such antagonists and whether, like rapprochement, leading to a cooling of the US-Russian relations, might similarly be for the US and Iran. So, what are the historic irritants driving our nations to be such antagonists? The relevant history goes back to the British role in the exploration and development of oil in Iran, which began in 1913. Over time Iran chafed at what it described as an unfair distribution of wealth from its oil fields. Mohammed Mossadegh, Iran's George Washington, a Ph.D. from Switzerland, campaigned on a platform of reforms and a pledge to nationalize Iran's oil resources.

Mossadegh was elected and nationalized the oil fields as he proposed. Great Britain sought to regain the lost footing by its CIA equivalent, fostering an unsuccessful coup attempt to overthrow Mossadegh. Shortly after that, in 1953, the US CIA, led by Kermit Roosevelt, the grandson of President Theodore Roosevelt, led a successful coup, with the same objective as Britain, and overthrew Mossadegh. They brought back foreign oil firms and placed Shah Mohammed Plaza over the reins in Iran.

The Shah, a friend to US interests despite implanting many reforms, was a divisive and cruel leader, guilty of many excesses, which led to the development of staunch opposition, especially from Islamic clerics who campaigned from abroad. Eventually, in 1979, the Shah abdicated, fled to exile in Egypt, under pressure, and the Islamic cleric Ruhollah Khomeini flew in from France and took over the government and formed the current Islamic republic.

Given the displeasure of many Iranians in the US role in over-throwing Mossadegh and installing the Shah and the US relations with the Shah, Iranian University students in 1979 rounded up over fifty members of the US embassy staff, holding them prisoner for 444 days. During President Jimmy Carter's term, a clandestine expedition was formed in 1980 to free the hostages. The expedition was ill-fated with invading aircraft colliding and burning during the planned operation. The prisoners were eventually released during the tenure of President Ronald Reagan.

Iran, under Islamic control, has been a bad actor on the inter-national scene, helping to prop up a dictatorial regime in Syria, fostering assassinations and efforts to overthrow governments, making it easy for any casual observer (and non-student of history) to suggest that one should not agree to treaties with such nations.

The reality is that peace treaties are generally between antag-onistic nations and are based on the hope of humankind to avert cataclysmic wars. For example, the US and the Soviet Union, at the height of the Cold War, mutually agreed to ban the testing of nuclear weapons.

All this is relevant history in explaining the schism between the US and Iran. Knowing this history, and comparison with the end of the Cold War would suggest the value of patience and time being allowed to cool passions and antagonisms between the two nations—what the Iran nuclear agreement would seem to make possible. But this history also suggests that a president must be aware of this history. The evidence seems to indicate that President Donald Trump does not read and is ignorant of history. The US abrogation of the Iran nuclear treaty, one can suggest, was a poor decision, ignorant of history, and not in the best interests of the US and the world, in general.

To make matters worse, Trump, after abrogating the treaty while facing worsened relations with Iran, threatened to destroy Iran and ordered US ships to fire on and destroy Iranian gunboats that tail US ships in gulf regions near Iran. It should be noted that all the other nations that were signatory to the treaty have chosen to remain in compliance and found Iran, until recently, to be complying.

The question is whether we, as a nation, believe that Trump alone possesses the wisdom and track record to abrogate a treaty that was so long in the making, involved our best and brightest minds, and similarly was viewed as in the best interests of the great list of signatory nations. Or was it just another whim of his in his anti-Obama syndrome? Of note is the fact Trump has proposed that former secretary of state, John Kerry, who worked tirelessly in helping to forge the agreement, be prosecuted for subsequent conversation with parties in Iran regarding the treaty abrogation. Trump, however, showed no such interest in prosecuting Michael Flynn for his conversations with Kislyak, which in principle was similarly a violation of the Logan Act.

5-3. The Paris Climate Agreement

In 1992, the year he was elected vice president of the United States, Senator Al Gore of Tennessee had already authored and published a book titled *Earth in the Balance*, in which he described the looming perils of global warming. The book and his efforts to alert the world community on the climate change challenge later led to Gore being awarded a Nobel Prize, in conjunction with the Intergovernmental Panel on Climate Change (IPCC). Gore was way ahead of the world in recognizing the looming crisis. In 2016, 196 countries reached and signed an agreement, meeting near Paris within the Framework Convention on Climate Change (UNFCC) dealing with greenhouse gas emissions mitigation, adaptation, and finance. The agreement has since been commonly referred to as the Paris Agreement.

The central goal of the agreement is to keep the long-term increase in global average temperature to well below two degrees centigrade. This objective is related to the risks of climate change affecting weather patterns, glacial melting, floods, and extremes in weather conditions overwhelmingly predicted as real by expert scientists throughout the world. The UNFCC[124] Report states that "The Paris Agreement requires that all parties put forward their best efforts through nationally determined contributions (NDCs) and to strengthen these efforts in the years ahead. This includes requirements that all parties report regularly on their emissions and their implementation efforts."

No mechanism forces a country to set a specific emissions target by a certain date. During the 2016 presidential campaign, Trump described global warming as "a hoax ... created by and for the Chinese to damage American trade," and promised, if elected, to withdraw the United States from the agreement. His tweets exhibit his naiveté on the topic during cold blasts, where he refers to "whatever happened to global warming?" showing his lack of understanding of weather and climate. Trump officially announced the planned US withdrawal from the accord in June 2017, an abrogation which cannot go into effect until November 2020.

5-4. Trump's Eviscerating of Environmental Rules

In May 2020, *the New York Times*[125] documented the full list of nearly 100 environmental rules that the Trump administration reversed. This effort compounds the harm done to the nation and the world by the abrogation of the Paris Climate agreement in that many of the rules impact greenhouse emissions. For example, *the Times* article states, "All told, the Trump administration's environmental rollbacks could significantly increase greenhouse emissions and lead to thousands of extra deaths from poor air quality each year according to energy and legal analysts."

As I read *the Times* article listing the 100 rollbacks, I focused on the one item, the reversal of rules spurred by the Deepwater Horizon oil spill. The impact of this oil spill was particularly damaging to an extended region in the Gulf of Mexico and contiguous landmasses in Louisiana and Mississippi. As a native of Louisiana, with extensive familiarity with the oil industry, I was struck the most by the reversal of rules seeking to reduce the likelihood of similar disasters. In 1956 and 1957, I was a student planning to obtain a degree in petroleum engineering.

For two different summers, I worked for oil field contracting companies to include working on a Gulf of Mexico oil platform (a so-called Texas Tower), laying oil pipelines in Louisiana marshes and clean up/reconstruction of oil platforms in Louisiana lakes. In the process, I experienced firsthand numerous incidents that could have caused death or severe injury.

My most graphic experience, which created my interest in the Horizon Deepwater spill, centered on my two-week role being a "go-fer" for the world-renowned oil well fire fighter, Red Adair. In the process of working a construction task replacing rotted wooden platforms surrounding oil field wells (so-called Christmas trees), a crane accident from our construction crew damaged a Christmas tree (owned by Hunt Oil Company), leading to the well-spewing oil and distillate in the air and throughout the lake.

Typically, such incidents routinely called in Red Adair, a famed well control specialist, to fly in from Texas to bring his unique expertise to controlling the spill (the so-called blowout). Red had only one associate, whose name was "Coots." And so, a fellow worker and I were recruited as helpers to work side-by-side with Red and Coots. (Of interest is that Coots was later to spin off his own company of oil well firefighters with a colleague named "Boots.")

In 1991, when the US military forced Sadam Hussein to retreat from his invasion of Kuwait, Hussein set fire to over 600 oil platforms. This new company, named "Coots and Boots," was credited with quelling the fires and plugging the leaks in a significant fraction of the burning sites. Throughout the two-week experience, the fear was that any spark could ignite the distillate vapor and engulf all of us in a fiery imbroglio.

As a result, only diesel-powered boats (no spark plugs) were allowed in the area. Red's expertise included dynamiting the Christmas tree's jagged remains to permit placement of a blowout preventer on the remaining huge pipe of 12-inch-or-so diameter. Getting a clean cut on the rough pipe-end was necessitated first by the construction of a small platform around the remains of the Christmas tree, followed by the four of us handling a large pipe cutter to obtain a clean pipe-end.

This entailed approximately a twenty-minute exposure (within 18-inch proximity) to the flowing well, with sand and oil distillate falling on our bodies and metal hats. I survived the experience and received a $150 bonus for exposure to the danger.

As it turned out, my career interest moved to physics and mathematics, away from petroleum engineering, primarily due to that experience. But the Deepwater Horizon oil spill brought back memories of working in Louisiana's oil fields. As the reports of the ecological disaster following that spill followed, it saddened me concerning the damage to an area near and dear to my heart, including the wildlife, fish, sea life, and estuary marshes.

Lombardo[126] has listed the many impacts of Deepwater Horizon's five-million-gallon oil spill into the Gulf of Mexico, describing it as the worst environmental disaster in the history of the United States, affecting marine life, tourism, and personal livelihoods. In addition to the eleven oil workers killed, the combination of the oil spilled and clean-up dispersants caused massive deformities in fish and crabs, killed over 400 dolphins, and added contaminants to food usually harvested from Gulf waters. Additionally, thousands of acres of marsh grasslands died, leading to permanent encroachment of the Gulf.

This recital suggests that any environmental regulations that work toward countering or reversing regulations that minimize the likelihood of future Deepwater Horizons should be made with utmost care and consideration. Lombardo's list of 100 Trump-initiated reversals of Obama era rules includes one such reversal, which is detailed by Davenport.[127] The rule change resulted from Trump naming a former oil lobbyist, David Bernhardt, as secretary of the interior. Davenport described the move as follows:

Among the safety changes put in place Thursday is a signif-icant reduction in the requirement for oil companies to test

118

fail-safe devices called blowout preventers, which are intended to be a last line of defense against disasters like Deepwater Horizon. In the 2010 fire and months-long oil leak, the failure of a blowout preventer, an immense device resting on the seabed and extremely difficult to access, was at the heart of the crisis.

In June 2019, Trump claimed[128] that the United States has "among the cleanest and sharpest air and water on earth." This was his explanation related to his abrogation of the Paris Agreement.

Fast forward to 2020. Amongst the many rollbacks and inaction of the EPA under Trump, one of the most egregious relates to the plight of the Chesapeake Bay—one of the nation's most important estuaries. As described by *Wikipedia*,[129] the bay has:

> Its northern portion in Maryland and the southern part in Virginia, the Chesapeake Bay, is a very important feature for the ecology and economy of those two states, as well as others surrounding within its watershed. More than 150 major rivers and streams flow into the Bay's 64,299-square-mile (166,534 km²) drainage basin, which covers parts of six states (New York, Pennsylvania, Delaware, Maryland, Virginia, and West Virginia) and all of Washington, DC / District of Columbia.

On May 19, 2020, the *Baltimore Sun Media Group*[130] reported that Maryland Attorney General Brian Frosh threatened the EPA with a lawsuit for its failure to enforce the nation's Clean Water Act, established in 1990. The Clean Water Act is described by *Wikipedia* as follows:

> The Clean Water Act (CWA) is the primary federal law in the United States governing water pollution. Its objective is to

restore and maintain the chemical, physical, and biological integrity of the nation's waters; recognizing the responsibilities of the states in addressing pollution and providing assistance to states to do so, including funding for publicly owned treatment works for the improvement of wastewater treatment; and maintaining the integrity of wetlands.

The Clean Water Act was one of the United States' first and most influential modern environmental laws. Its laws and regulations are primarily administered by the US Environmental Protection Agency (EPA) in coordination with state governments, though some of its provisions, such as those involving filling or dredging, are administered by the US Army Corps of Engineers.

At issue is the fact that the states adjoining Maryland and Virginia introduce trash and pollutants into the rivers and streams that empty into the Chesapeake Bay. Anyone traveling over the Conowingo Dam near where the Chesapeake River empties into the Chesapeake Bay near Havre de Grace, Maryland, can attest to this. Pictures of the accumulation of tons of trash and pollutants at the dam's entrance should be Exhibit 1 in Maryland's threatened lawsuit.

On May 28, 2020, the *Wall Street Journal* published an article titled "States Sue over Easing of Emission Standards."[131] The article stated, "A coalition of twenty-three states filed suit against the Trump administration's March easing of tail-pipe emissions standards, arguing it violated the law and was based on faulty analysis."

The standards being reversed had been put in place by the Obama administration in 2012 to reduce greenhouse gas emissions and improve fuel efficiency. And so, again, the citizenry must ask, where do Trump's interests lie, how informed is he, how much does he read, and what experts does he consult before significant decisions are made? The answer seems to be in the negative on all counts. Additionally, one must ask, how many of Trump's initiatives are merely part of his anti-Obama syndrome?

Chapter 6

Trump's Lies Are His Modus Operandi

6-1. Trump: Lying is a Daily Occurrence

The Trump presidency will go down in history as unparalleled concerning a daily litany of lies and mischaracterizations. Many of his lies were/are in making false claims about various aspects of his success in office or his alleged need to correct the ills he attributed to predecessors. Trump's lies are so frequent, so repetitive, many of which deal with matters of great national import and presidential responsibilities, that tagging him with the term "Prevaricator in Chief" is appropriate.

Prevarication is a more formal way of saying some statement made is a "lie" and of substance in its misrepresentation. For example, *Webster's* dictionary (1913 edition) definition of prevarication is "a secret abuse in the exercise of public office" is most appropriate for Trump because of the import of his lies on a sizable portion of the public and the public's understanding of public policy issues.

Glenn Kessler of *the Washington Post* has kept an on-going tab of Trump's false or misleading claims (lies) by giving "Pinocchios," dependent on the degree of falsity. On April 14, 2020, after Trump had been in office 1,170 days, Kessler, Rizzo, and Kelly[132] totaled the number at 18,000 false or misleading claims.

Leonhardt,[133] of *the New York Times*, went beyond the mere lies to chronicle Trump's actions (and inactions) in office under the title "Donald Trump versus the United States (just the facts in forty sentences)." Leonhardt begins the list of forty with "pressuring a foreign leader to interfere in the 2020 election" and ends with "he is the president of the United States, and he is a threat to virtually everything that the United States should stand for."

Throughout his presidency, Trump has continued his pre-election penchant for lying, big and small, essentially seeking daily to conceal or deny any mishaps, conceal or avoid responsibility for actions that were in his purview, exaggerating and lying about his accomplishments—all to prop up his ego and chances for re-election continually. This chapter will chronicle his lies about "the greatest economy ever," how China has paid the US for his tariffs and concealed the fact that funds for the payoff to farmers, necessitated by the tariffs, came from the US Treasury and not the Chinese.

Johnson[134] describes Trump's penchant for lying as a part of his then "business" persona—contained in Trump's book—co-authored with Tony Schwarz titled *The Art of the Deal*, which was published in 1987.

It's an innocent form of exaggeration—and a very effective form of promotion. The final key to the way I promote is bravado. I play to people's fantasies. People may not always think big themselves, but they can still get very excited by those who do. That's why a little hyperbole never hurts. People want to believe something is the biggest and the greatest and the most spectacular. I call it truthful hyperbole.

As an example of this hyperbole, Trump regularly laces his pronouncements, no matter how routine, with expressions such as *greatest, outstanding, best, beautiful, time will tell*. Similarly, he has ingrained in his subordinates the need for their continually describing his actions and decisions with similar expressions of grandeur, as exhibited during an early press exposure of his cabinet where every member, in sequence, paid homage to his greatness—except for Tillerson and Mattis, who thought the ritual was unseemly. Trump's litany of outright lies, as described in Chapter 1, began before his run for the presidency. They included:

- Claiming to be the top graduate at the Wharton School, University of Pennsylvania;
- Calling reporters claiming to be "John Baron;"
- Claiming to have bone spurs to avoid the military draft;
- Describing his inheritance as only one million dollars and saying that it was repaid;
- The claim to *Forbes* concerning his net worth; and
- Lying about the pedigree/experience of the Trump University instructors/lecturers.

One of his first whoppers that gained national attention was his "birtherism claim" that Barack Obama was born in Kenya and was not eligible to run for president. During the 2016 presidential campaign, despite all recent presidential candidates releasing their income tax filings, Trump claimed he could not do so because he was under audit.

There was/is no such IRS restriction, and, in fact, Richard Nixon released his taxes despite being under audit. Federal law mandates that the Treasury Department must turn over a president's taxes to the Ways and Means Committee if requested in the context of the committee's duties in forging legislation. In 2019, the committee did request the Trump tax returns, but Trump's treasury secretary, Mnuchin, refused. It became a litigious issue now before the Supreme Court.

In April 2019, the treasury inspector general (IG) ruled that the treasury secretary had correctly acted in handing and refusing the request. In what has become a pattern, this ruling came only days after Trump had fired two inspector generals for *"disloyalty."* By mid-May 2020, Trump had additionally fired two other IG's and numerous other high-level officials ostensibly for nothing other than "disloyalty."

Similarly, the state of New York requested tax data from Deutsche Bank, Trump's primary lender, for many of his real estate projects. Once again, Trump contested the request, and recently the Supreme Court ruled that the president had no special privilege and that the records must be provided to prosecutors. As is his usual, Trump has appealed this decision. The importance of these records is highlighted by Trump's attorney, Michael Cohen, testifying before Congress that "Trump routinely deflated the valuation of his properties for tax purposes and inflated their value for lending/collateral purposes."

Other pending lawsuits include issues of Trump allegedly violating the "Emoluments Clause," which prohibits presidents from receiving monetary benefits from foreign sources. Questions on this topic stem from foreigners staying at the Trump Washington Hotel and Trump's scheduling the next G-7 meeting at the Trump Mar-A-Largo resort in Florida, which was canceled after his staff convinced him this was not very wise.

Before the election, Trump pledged to divest himself of properties that created conflicts under the Emoluments Clause—an issue he "skirted" by having his children manage the subject properties. Another issue before the courts involves Trump's alleged "hush money," $130,000 payment made before the election to porn star

Stormy Daniels to which Trump's attorney Michael Cohen has admitted. Trump subsequently repaid Cohen. Initially, Trump not only denied the affair but also denied the payoff. Trump's new attorney, Rudy Giuliani, later confirmed the payoff.[135]

A significant news item during the election was the Trump Tower meeting between Donald Trump Jr. and Russian operatives alleging to have dirt on Hillary Clinton. Trump, to this day, denies having been informed of this meeting and having crafted verbiage describing the purpose of the meeting to the press. The conventional wisdom is that Don Jr. would not hold such a meeting without first notifying his father, and phone records show a phone call (likely from Don Jr.) to an unregistered phone number before the meeting.

After the election, Trump quickly followed with another "untruthful hyperbole" that the networks had understated the size of his inauguration crowd size. Within days, Trump's press secretary, Sean Spicer, quickly followed his boss's exaggeration with a flat out lie about Trump's inauguration crowd size (to which Spicer later admitted his regret). He described Trump's inauguration crowd size as[136] "the largest audience to ever witness an inauguration, period, both in-person and around the globe."

For his untruths, half-truths, and outright lies, describing Trump as the "Prevaricator in Chief" is appropriate.

6-2. Trump's Claims of Widespread Voter Fraud

As the coronavirus spread and the country came to a stand-still, several state elections were affected, including Wisconsin and Alaska. There was widespread concern that the need for and benefit of "social distancing" would be significantly compromised by the traditional voting process. Numerous states quickly gained approval (within their state) for voting to be done by mail-in balloting—others moved the elections forward to a more distant date. The result was that the national discussion for adopting "mail-in-balloting" everywhere, including the upcoming 2020 presidential election, became a front and center topic.

Trump quickly weighed in, stating his objection to mail-in balloting. After the 2016 election, Trump, with no proof at all, claimed that Clinton's near three million popular vote win was due to voter fraud—in particular in California. This claim led to Trump naming Kris Kobach (as described in Chapter 3) to head an ill-fated "Voter Fraud Commission," which was quickly abandoned because its premise was based on lies. As this latter issue of mail-in balloting has (in the COVID-19 aftermath) come under increasing discussion and likelihood, Trump quickly weighed-in with, "Tremendous potential for voter fraud, for whatever reason, doesn't work out well for Republican."[137] Trump's latest position, in late July of 2020, with no basis in fact, is that mail-in balloting will be ripe for fraud. Rather than initiate efforts to expedite mail-in balloting, to save lives by avoiding the exposure of voters to COVID-19, he has suggested delaying the election.

In consonance with these actions, voter ID laws, championed by Kris Kobach in Kansas, suffered another blow in April 2020, when the Tenth Circuit Court[138] ruled that Kansas "proof of citizenship law indisputably has disenfranchised approximately 30,000 would-be Kansas voters."

The court found that there was insufficient proof that significant voter fraud existed and found that in nineteen years, only sixty-seven non-citizens registered or tried to register in Kansas. Administrative anomalies could account for the presence of many, or even most, of the sixty-seven cases.

This ruling was similar to that in Texas, where in January 2019, the Texas Secretary of State David Whitley[139] released a bombshell that hit the national news claiming that 95,000 registered voters in Texas had questionable citizenship. Like many such previous claims, including those by Kris Kobach and Trump, further scrutiny showed this claim to be false. The Texas Secretary of State's Office eventually walked back the finding after an embarrassing review of the data revealed that tens of thousands of the voters flagged were citizens and, after study, found that no evidence of large scale voter fraud had emerged. As his wont, Trump jumped on the initial report and tweeted:

"58,000 non-citizens voted in Texas, with 95,000 non-citizens registered to vote. These numbers are just the tip of the iceberg. All over the country, especially in California, voter fraud is rampant. Must be stopped. Strong voter ID!"! @foxandfriends

Nevertheless, Trump, despite his claims of widespread voter fraud having been disproved, including his claim that illegal voting in California resulted in his losing the popular vote to Clinton by 2. 9 million votes, continues to harp on this topic. He disdains to look ahead at efforts (and Congressional legislation) to develop a rational procedure for the November 2020 election that minimizes widespread virus exposure and/or greatly reduced numbers of voters. Commenting on this look ahead initiative, Trump observed to Fox and Friends, "if you'd ever agreed to it, you'd never have a Republican elected in this country again."

Trump's fixation on the lie of voter fraud led to his threatening to withhold unspecified federal funds for Michigan and Nevada[140] over absentee, mail-in voting. Michigan's secretary of state had announced a plan to send absentee ballot "applications" to all of its 7.7 million voters for the state's primary election in August and general elections in November. As often his custom of "shoot first and ask questions later," Trump erroneously described the Michigan action in his tweet:

Breaking: Michigan sends absentee ballot to 7.7 million people ahead of Primaries and the General Election: This was done illegally and without authorization by a rogue Secretary of State. I will ask to hold up funding to Michigan if they want to go down this Voter Fraud path.

In this tweet, Trump incorrectly refers to "ballots" rather than "applications for ballots." Michigan Secretary of State Jocelyn Benson responded by tweet noting that she had a name and said:

It's Jocelyn Benson ... And we sent applications, not ballots. Just like my GOP colleagues in Iowa, Georgia, Nebraska, and West Virginia.

Benson's action, like that of so many other state officials nationwide, was a prudent planning action for an alternative to traditional voting methods in anticipation of continued likelihood of COVID-19 contagion by closely gathered voters.

6-3. Trump's Litany of Prevarication (Lies)

The whopper, preceding Barack Obama's successful presidential campaign, was that Obama was born in Kenya, was thus not eligible to be president, that Trump had proof of same and had dispatched someone to Hawaii to acquire documentation. Later, after much embarrassment and Obama providing evidence of his Hawaii birth, Trump blamed Hillary Clinton for first suggesting Obama's Kenyan birth. Trump never disclosed the promised findings of the operative he claimed to have dispatched to Hawaii.

As stated earlier, Trump's daily lies have led to a cottage industry of "fact-checkers." Trump has seldom been confronted with questions about his lies. Still, on rare occasions where a question has been posed to him that implies negativity of one of his actions or inactions, he has browbeaten the questioner, described the subject question as "fake news" or "nasty" and put down the questioner's competence, describing his/her publication, TV or radio outlet as effectively a losing organization, e.g., "the failing *New York Times*." Similarly, Trump has carried on a vendetta with Jeff Bezos, founder, and majority stockholder in Amazon, because Bezos owns *the Washington Post*, which has won several Pulitzer Prizes in covering Trump, including David Fahrenthold's exposure on the Trump charities as described in Chapter 1. This vendetta has led to:

a) An ongoing lawsuit over Trump's alleged interference in the Defense Department contract known as JEDI[141] (which was awarded to Microsoft); and

b) Trump's pressuring the Postal Service to increase rates on delivery of Amazon products.[142] The lie here is that Trump refuses to admit/recognize that the Postal Service deficit is due to the law that forces the Postal Service to set aside funds annually to pre-fund its pension system for seventy-five years.

Trump has abandoned the long-held tradition of a frequent, sometimes daily news conference by presidential press secretaries. For example, in April 2020, his press secretary, Stephanie Grisham, who had held the position for almost a year before being replaced in April 2020, had never held a press conference. Earlier, Kellyanne Conway, a former campaign manager and key staffer, coined the term "alternative facts." Sarah Huckabee Sanders, who had the longest tenure at the position, apologized for wrongly stating why Trump had fired FBI Director James Comey.

By contrast, during the COVID-19 crisis of 2020, Trump has personally held an almost daily press conference featuring himself. At one of these early April sessions, Jonathan Karl, the highly respected ABC news chief and Washington correspondent, co-anchor of "This Week With George Stephanopoulos," and president of the White House Correspondents Association asked the president about one of his COVID-19 actions/inactions. Trump belittled the question and responded[143] by calling the newsman a "third-rate reporter" who "will never make it."

Goldberg,[144] commenting on these daily Trump-led COVID-19 press conferences, which were accompanied by health policy and science experts Dr. Anthony Fauci and Dr. Deborah Birx who both walked a tightrope in correcting Trump's statements, commented:

> Still, it is beyond outrageous that Americans have to witness the spectacle of public health officials tailoring their responses to questions so as not to offend the president … It's even worse that we have to put up with a president who answers questions off the cuff without regard for facts or concerns for how what he is saying might be misinterpreted. Add in his incessant dedication to petty grievances, partisan puffery, and chest-beating braggadocio, along with all the obligatory obsequiousness he requires of officials who know far more than he does. Together these things create an affirmative need to call out the nonsense because the nonsense isn't just annoying, it's dangerous.

In May 2020, while visiting the Lincoln Memorial in Washington, Trump stated, "I am greeted with a hostile press, the likes of which no president has ever seen. The closest would be that gentleman right up there. They always said, 'Lincoln — nobody got treated worse than Lincoln.' I believe I am treated worse."

Dana Milbank,[145] a columnist for *the Washington Post* who frequently writes satirically, has penned a most amusing article commenting on Trump's claim. He begins his article by listing a trove of grossly negative comments (about an unnamed president) where the reader not familiar with Milbank's writings would conclude, in reading the beginning of the article, that the list proves Trump's point about his terrible treatment by the press. The perceptive reader, however, familiar with Milbank's humor, quickly suspects that this most atrocious list was historically written about Lincoln, and reading to the end quickly finds this to be true—thus proving that once again, Trump is a prevaricator extraordinaire.

In May and June 2020, Trump seemed to top himself with both the pettiness and viciousness of his lies. First, there was his pushing the conspiracy theory that MSNBC Morning Joe host Joe Scarborough was a suspect in the murder of one of Scarborough's aides when he was a Florida congressman.[146] The former aide's husband wrote a deeply moving letter to Twitter Chief Executive Officer Jack Dorsey asking him to delete tweets by President Trump furthering a baseless conspiracy theory about his wife's death. His letter to Dorsey included:

> I'm asking you to intervene in this instance because the President of the United States has taken something that does not belong to him—the memory of my dead wife—and perverted it for perceived political gain. My wife deserves better.

Then there was the petty lie denying that he was forced to take residence in the bunker below the White House during the George Floyd murder protests. Trump claimed he was merely inspecting the bunker, but Attorney General Barr claimed otherwise.[147]

On June 9, Trump tweeted the conspiracy theory[148] that was pushed on the OAN Network, his new favorite over Fox, that a seventy-five-year-old man who was pushed, knocked down, and severely injured during the George Floyd Buffalo protests was an Antifa agent provocateur.

6-4. Trump's Prevarication on Tariffs

Few would dispute the fact that the Chinese play hardball in trade policies. The result has been that there is a large imbalance in the value of goods bought by the US from China compared to the value of goods sold by the US to China. Seldom mentioned, in particular by Trump, however, is that for services, the balance is significantly in favor of the US. The whole issue of trade imbalance and tariffs is complicated and is multinational, affecting many different nations in many different ways.

Accordingly, trade agreements have frequently and generally been negotiated as multinational so that the various trading partners' conflicting issues can somehow be negotiated and, in effect, compromises are made to avert unending trade wars. Such was the case for agreements such as NAFTA, which involved the US, Canada, and Mexico. Amadeo,[149] in an article titled "Tariffs Explained with an Example," makes clear that US consumers of goods imported from China pay the tariff, not China, as Trump continually repeats.

> Tariffs increase the price of the import. For example, on March 1, 2018, President Trump announced he would impose a 25% tariff on steel imports and a 10% tariff on aluminum ... the tariff has and will raise costs for steel users, like automakers. And they'll pass that onto consumers ... Tariffs are taxes paid

by consumers of imported goods. These raise prices of goods brought in from another country.

Werschkul[150] has documented that Trump has lied about who pays for tariffs at least 108 times in 2019. Trump's own economic advisor Larry Kudlow, in an interview with Chris Wallace of Fox,[151] acknowledged that when China exports products hit by tariffs to the United States, it is the US importer who pays the tariff—not the Chinese.

6-5. Trump's Prevarication on the "Greatest Economy Ever, Best Job Growth, Lowest Unemployment, Best Wages"

Goldberg's description[144] of Trump's "partisan puffery, and chest-beating braggadocio" is exemplified by the president's frequent reference to his having brought to and presided over the country's best and greatest economy, job growth, lowest unemployment, and best wages. Robert Reich is a professor, economist, editor, publisher of eighteen books, and former labor secretary who has served under both Republican and Democratic presidents. He has addressed these lies in an article titled "Trump's 4 Biggest Lies about Today's Economy."[152] In each subtopic, Professor Reich provides historical counterexamples putting the lie to Trump's chest-beating braggadocio.

6-6. The Lie about who Pays for Farm Subsidies

One of the effects of Trump's tariffs thus far has been Chinese retaliation by their cessation of purchasing US farm crops, in particular billions of dollars of soybeans. In response, Trump has provided many billion dollars in farm aid to farmers poorly affected by the lost Chinese market. Throughout, Trump has implied that these farm subsidies were paid for by the Chinese through tariffs that he imposed. This, of course, is a lie because, as detailed above, tariffs were funded by US consumers. As of December 2019, the cost of Trump's farm bailout was $28 billion,[153] which is more than double the cost of the auto bailout that Republicans opposed.

6-7. The Lie that Led to Impeachment

On December 18, 2019, Donald J. Trump was impeached by the United States House of Representatives on two charges of abuse of power and obstruction of Congress.

The abuse of power charge centered on his alleged solicitation of Ukrainian President Volodymyr Zelensky to help his re-election bid by investigating his likely rival, Joe Biden, and Biden's son Hunter. The so-called quid pro quo resulted from a phone conversation between Zelensky and Trump that was both preceded and followed by back-channel communication to the Ukrainian leader that a requested formal meeting between Trump and Zelensky and commencement of the US military aid to Ukraine were dependent on the subject investigation by Ukraine.

Throughout the period preceding and during the impeachment, Trump continually referred to the written transcription of the conversation (that was made public) as being "perfect"—in effect, denying there was a quid pro quo. A special classification shielded public release of the actual recording of the conversation. Numerous officials testified before and during the formal House of Representatives impeachment hearing, attesting to the fact that there was the quid pro quo. Several of the aides who so testified were subsequently fired for "disloyalty."

The obstruction charge centered on the allegation that Trump obstructed the inquiry by telling his administration officials to ignore subpoenas for documents and testimony. The Senate trial was marked by the Senate's total refusal to hear any evidence on the subject charges and led to a quick acquittal vote.

As a resident of Maryland, as it relates to the historic incident I describe below, it seems appropriate to contrast the Trump impeachment hearings with the impeachment actions that were underway leading to Nixon's resignation. In Trump's case, no Republican senators, except for Mitt Romney of Utah, were of the bent to air any of Trump's transgressions that were at issue in the House impeachment hearings. As a result, there were no Senate impeachment hearings—just the final vote. As Nixon's Watergate transgressions were being debated in the House of Representatives, several aides were willing to lie to cover up the wrongdoings. In the Nixon hearings in the House Judiciary Committee, only one courageous Republican congressman, Lawrence J. Hogan of Maryland, was willing to stand on principle. Hogan was the only Republican on the committee to vote for all three articles of impeachment against Nixon when they were adopted in committee. Hogan famously said into the television cameras:[154]

> The thing that's so appalling to me is that the president, when this whole idea was suggested to him, didn't, in righteous indignation, rise up, and say, 'Get out of here, you're in the office of the President of the United States. How can you talk about blackmail and bribery and keeping witnesses silent? This is the Presidency of the United States.' But my President didn't do that. He sat there, and he worked and worked to try to cover this thing up so it wouldn't come to light.

Hogan's principled stand deflected his career trajectory as a Maryland elected official, but history has honored him for his integrity. In 2014, his son, Lawrence J. Hogan Jr., was elected as the sixty-second governor of Maryland. He was reelected in 2018.

6-8. Trump's Nicknames for those he Perceives as "Antagonists"

During the campaign of 2015 and 2016 and his presidency, Trump disparaged his opponents with negative, frequently ugly nicknames to an extent never seen before in US political campaigns.[155] Words he used in describing those who have crossed him include "scum" and "treasonous."

Chapter 7

Coronavirus Was Trump's Cuban Missile Crisis—He Failed Us Miserably

7-1. Early Concerns about Trump's Leadership

This chapter chronicles Trump's most significant challenge (and most consequential failure) in mishandling the coronavirus pandemic, leading to countless deaths that could have been avoided with more skillful presidential leadership. The pandemic is described herein as Trump's "equivalent Cuban Missile Crisis"—a precedent which any president schooled in history would have been well-advised to learn from.

The Cuban Missile Crisis served as a historical example of the wisdom of an early convening of a brain trust of key, expert advisors to craft a path forward and do so, in this case, based on science and logic. An early concern of Trump's cabinet officers is described below where the president's lack of inclination (and necessary knowledge) in preparation for such a strategy, in any future crisis, was anticipated, but with a grossly unsatisfactory outcome.

The book titled *A Very Stable Genius* by Rucker and Leonnig[156] describes how Trump's secretary of defense, General Jim Mattis, secretary of state, Rex Tillerson, and director of the National

138

Economic Council, Gary Cohn, during Trump's second year in office, were quite concerned about Trump's overall understanding of the world we live in—in the military forces and nations that wished us evil. Accordingly, the three cabinet officers (joined by the chairman of the Joint Chiefs of Staff, General Joseph Dunford at the meeting), planned a major briefing at the Pentagon in the historic room known as the Tank, usually reserved for meetings of major consequence including discussion of military tactics, "where the joint chiefs decide on grave matters that could send young men and women to their deaths."

Rucker and Leonnig describe how:

The group had grown alarmed over the first six months of the Trump administration by gaping holes on the president's knowledge of history and of the alliances forged at the end of World War II that served as the foundation of America's strength in the world. Trump had unnerved trusted friends by dismissing existing relations with Western democracies as worthless, including by questioning the value of NATO while cultivating friendlier ones with Russia.

The group was further concerned about the president's impulsive ideas and his many gaps in understanding world affairs. On July 20, 2017, the group invited Trump to the Tank for what they planned as "a tutorial on the state of the world."

The objective was to essentially give Trump a briefing with emphasis on military posture—friend and foe alike. The meeting quickly turned into a Trump tantrum. During this fiasco, he belittled the generals as "losers," complained about the cost of alliances, and essentially confirmed for the meeting organizers the fear that prompted the briefing. It should be noted that Cohn, Mattis, and Tillerson are no longer in the administration. Incidents such as this are what has led to reports that two former cabinet officers separately were quoted as describing Trump as a "moron" and "idiot."

The need for the Tank briefing was consistent, especially as Trump's presidency unfolded, with his well-publicized penchant for not being a reader, having a lack of knowledge on history, and his disdain for detailed briefings. Barnes and Goldman of *the New York Times*[157] described how Trump blamed others for his flawed response to the coronavirus, including China, governors, the Obama administration, the World Health Organization, and a low-level analyst who delivers his intelligence briefings. They pointed out, however, that he received warnings about the growing threat from higher-ranking officials, epidemiologists, scientists, biodefense officials, and other national security aides.

Based on interviews with ten current and former intelligence officials, Barnes and Goldman pointed out that the problem seems to be that Trump "is difficult to brief on critical security matters … veers off on tangents … has a short attention span and rarely if ever reads intelligence reports."

Conservative lawyer George Conway, husband of Kellyanne Conway, Trump's campaign manager and now close aide, in a Twitter account,[158] has chronicled Trump's numerous gaffes regarding countries, cities, geography, and related history. A typical example includes a Trump exchange with the Indian Prime Minister Modi, where Trump stated, "It's not like you've got China on your border."

And so, it turned out that Trump's greatest crisis, and one at which he failed, was not related to defense but rather the world-wide coronavirus pandemic which came to be known as COVID-19, the disease caused by a virus. As the crisis unfolded, Trump's failure to take the badly needed, timely, and effective leadership to save as many lives as possible was chronicled by an ever-vigilant press corps, as described herein.

On April 14, 2020, Trump told the country, in his daily coronavirus update, that he alone had the authority to "reopen the country," and that he alone would exercise that authority. A hue and cry came from many governors and constitutional scholars. On April 15, in the next day's briefing, he reversed himself, without admitting his reversal, and indicated the governors would provide the timing and details of the country reopening. Then, on May 22, 2020, as the nation and the governors wrestled with varying coronavirus conditions, he reversed himself again by demanding that governors allow churches to open immediately by stating,[159] "If they don't do it, I will override the governors. America, we need more prayer, not less." This writer concludes that Trump's mishandling of the coronavirus pandemic was his most significant (and most consequential) failure up to this point in time.

7-2. The Lesson that Could Have Been Learned from the Cuban Missile Crisis

One of the early pre-election fears I had about a possible Trump presidency had its roots in my brief career stint as an Army officer. During my two years as a technical project officer (2nd and 1st Lt.), I was stationed at Aberdeen Proving Ground, Maryland (APG). One of the occasional extra duties was to serve as the nighttime staff duty officer (SDO). This added duty rotated among the young officers stationed on the base, with the assignments revolving separately for weeknights and weekend nights. The assignment was to serve as the "ears" of the Proving Ground. Any unusual, untoward, or hazardous emergency event that occurred, during the night, over the many acres, many activities, and thousands of personnel of the Proving Ground, would be called into a more senior staff duty officer. The junior SDOs, like me, had a booklet of standard operating procedures, specifying who was to be notified

141

(a more senior officer) and who was to be called the "action" officer for unusual occurrences. As luck would have it, during the two weeks of the Cuban Missile Crisis, within three days or so, I had both the weekday and weekend duty.

Aberdeen, then and now, is host to many major Army agencies, including the world headquarters of the Army's Test and Evaluation Command (TECOM). During my first of two nights during the Cuban Missile Crisis, the nation was apprised of the fact that the Soviet Union had installed nuclear missiles in Cuba and that major US cities, for the first time, were in reach of missile-borne nuclear weapons. The US military, in such circumstances, goes on alert using criteria known as Defense Condition or DEFCON. In this instance, all US military agencies worldwide were instructed to assume (or go on alert) and/or make preparations under the specification known as DEFCON 3. Wikipedia defines DEFCON as follows:

> The defense readiness condition (DEFCON) is an alert state used by the United States Armed Forces. The DEFCON system was developed by the Joint Chiefs of Staff (JCS) and unified and specified combatant commands. It prescribes five graduated levels of readiness (or states of alert) for the US military. It increases in severity from DEFCON 5 (least severe) to DEFCON 1 (most severe) to match varying military situations.

During my SDO stint, during the first night of the Cuban Missile Crisis, the worldwide subagencies of TECOM, per standard orders, notified their parent headquarters at Aberdeen that they had assumed and were in DEFCON 3. At night, the standard instruction for these agencies was to call the APG SDO, which turned out to be me. I, in turn, made a note of the agency's DEFCON 3 posture, and followed up by notifying the more senior SDO, who similarly had duty but was allowed to serve his/her nighttime tour at home, so long as he was available by phone.

The coronavirus crisis similarity in consequence (and need for presidential leadership), to the Cuban Missile Crisis, is exemplified by an alert issued by the National Center for Medical Intelligence (NCMI) before March 1, 2020. The NCMI raised the risk of a pandemic warning. It went from WATCHCON 2, a probable crisis, to WATCHCON 1, an imminent crisis, due to sustained human-to-human transmission outside of China.[160] Understanding the similarity of the need for wise presidential action in this crisis to that of the Cuban Missile Crisis requires a brief historical note.

The background of the events leading to the Cuban Missile Crisis began with the incident known as the ill-fated Bay of Pigs. During the Kennedy administration, a group of Cuban exiles, trained and nurtured by the US military and CIA, went ashore in Cuba and rather than generating the hoped-for insurrection that might overthrow the Fidel Castro regime, were defeated by Cuban forces at the Bay of Pigs. Cuba, then and now, was a surrogate of the Soviet Union (now Russia), and at the time, Nikita Khrushchev was the Soviet leader. The placement of Soviet missiles in Cuba was the Soviet's (and Cuba's) way to thwart another US effort, such as that at the Bay of Pigs, to invade Cuba to overthrow Castro.

The immediate US reaction, bolstered by public opinion, was that the nuclear missile presence aimed at the US, so close to the continental US, was intolerable. President John F. Kennedy, the Joint Chiefs, Secretary of Defense Robert McNamara, and key senior military and diplomatic strategists were quickly convened into strategic discussions as to what to do about the threat.

The impasse lasted thirteen days and was finally settled as follows: Khrushchev eventually sent Kennedy two letters of differing tones—one belligerent, the other, less belligerent. One suggested that the thorn in the Soviet side (and Cuba's) was the prevention of another US invasion force such as the Bay of Pigs. Also, the Soviets' second thorn was the US-NATO Jupiter nuclear missiles in Turkey adjacent to the Soviet Union. The crisis eventually ended when the US blockaded Cuba (ironically, called a quarantine), preventing further missile shipments, and eventually agreed not to invade Cuba again—and the nuclear missiles were withdrawn from Cuba.

The second part of the agreement, deemed politically sensitive in the US, was to remove the Jupiter missiles in Turkey—a component of the agreement that was kept secret at the time. The movie *Thirteen Days*[161] depicts the different options that were presented to President Kennedy. Among the possibilities seriously advanced (as proposed by the military advisors) was the bombing of the missile sites, followed by an invasion force. Kennedy feared this would lead to a Soviet invasion of West Berlin and further escalation. The movie depicts intense deliberations by military and diplomatic experts, including discussion of likely consequences that could arise from the alternatives that were in serious consideration.

Historically, the Cuban Missile Crisis, the deliberations and decision process leading to the ultimate and very satisfactory solution, is an example for any president not only to be aware of but also to be guided by. For example, in the process of seeking the best advice available during the crisis, Kennedy consulted with three former presidents: Herbert Hoover, Dwight Eisenhower, and Harry Truman, along with former Secretary of State Dean Acheson. By contrast, Brower[162] in describing an interview with Trump wrote:

I asked President Trump if his years behind the storied Resolute desk had made him empathize with his predecessors. In the

144

very room where most of them had called on one another in times of crisis for years—and well before the novel coronavirus pandemic changed the country, and the world—Mr. Trump was dismissive of the men who came before him. He answered my question without hesitation: "No, no." His attitude toward his predecessors has apparently only hardened over time. The chaos of the pandemic has shined a spotlight on his contempt for the living presidents. He has stripped them of one of their traditional jobs in retirement: their unique ability to unify the country in a crisis. The relative absence of Barack Obama, George W. Bush, Bill Clinton, and Jimmy Carter is more striking now than ever before.

As one who lived through this time, with the stimulus provided by being the SDO, my long career with the Army and defense issues, and my lifelong interest in history and world affairs, the question of anyone with the fitness to handle a major crisis such as the Cuban Missile Crisis was paramount in my assessment of presidential candidates. I assessed that Donald Trump did not have the background, temperament, knowledge, or judgment for convening and leading a team of experts to handle such a crisis. He was and has been continually characterized as one who is not a student of history.

7-3. Coronavirus (COVID-19) was Trump's Equivalent of the Cuban Missile Crisis

In January 2020, the world became aware that there was a spreading virus known as the coronavirus, or COVID-19, that was spreading in the Wuhan Province of China. The likelihood of this becoming a worldwide concern became quickly known, as evident later, by three Republican and one Democratic

US senator (Burr, Loeffler, Inhofe, and Feinstein) who unloaded several million dollars in stocks in anticipation of the economic shock to the stock market.

Trump's various comments and cognizant failures on the coming pandemic are listed by Mangan[163] and by Stevens and Tan.[164] For example, Mangan quotes CNBC's Joe Kernan asking Trump on January 22, 2020, "Are there worries about a pandemic at this point?"

Trump's answer was, "No, not at all … It's one person coming in from China."

Trump's various early statements as listed by Steven and Tan included:

- January 22: "We have it totally under control."
- February 10: "Looks like by April, you know, in theory, when it gets a little warmer, it miraculously goes away."
- February 24: "The coronavirus is very much under control in the USA.… Stock Market starting to look very good to me."
- March 24: "I'd love to have the country opened up and just raring to go by Easter."

Trump's failure to grasp the enormity of the problem and his failure to have and seek the judgment by scientists, and the scientific evidence, was expressed by Leonhardt:[165]

> The inconsistent and sometimes outright incorrect information coming from the White House has left Americans unsure of what, if anything, to do. By early March, experts were already arguing for aggressive measures to slow the virus's spread and avoid overwhelming the medical system. The presidential bully pulpit could have focused people on the need to change

their behavior in a way that no private citizen could have. Trump could have specifically encouraged older people—at most risk from the virus—to be careful. Once again, he chose not to take action.

Lipton and five *New York Times* colleagues[166] did a most intensive analysis of Trump's inactions during the unfolding virus catastrophe, and the various official studies and related high-level documentation that was available to him in the unfolding January to March 2020 timeframe. Unlike the Cuban Missile Crisis, where President Kennedy quickly gathered a crisis team to assess the threat, lay out options and act, Trump not only acted sparingly but ignored the official studies that were explicitly done for presidential attention. *The New York Times* team led by Lipton found the following:

- Mr. Trump repeatedly played down the seriousness of the virus and focused on other issues.
- He focused instead on controlling the message, protecting gains in the economy.
- The inaction was complicated by a long-running dispute inside the administration on how to deal with China.
- His response was colored by his suspicion of the "Deep State."

The well-known fact that the president does not read but spends a lot of time on Twitter, golfing, watching TV, and has a low tolerance for detailed briefings is borne out by the list of high-level studies and advice, listed by Lipton and his colleagues, that would normally be the basis for presidential attention and call to action, including:

- The National Security Council office … received intelligence reports in early January predicting the spread of the virus to the United States … and was raising options like keeping Americans home from work and shutting down cities the size of Chicago.

- Despite Mr. Trump's denial weeks later, he was told at the time about a January 29 memo produced by his trade adviser, Peter Navarro, laying out in striking detail the potential risks of a coronavirus pandemic: as many as half a million deaths and trillions of dollars in economic losses.

- In a January 30 call from his human services secretary, Alex M. Azar II, which Trump described as "alarmist," Mr. Trump was warned directly of the possibility of a pandemic.

- A plan announced by Mr. Azar establishing a "surveillance" enabling the measurement of the next hot spots was delayed for weeks with a similar delay in developing a testing capability—inhibiting insight into the spread of the virus.

- By the third week in February, social distancing and staying home from work were recommended to Trump. Additional weeks went by before reluctant acceptance and an unchecked spread of the virus.

- As noted earlier, before March 1, the NCMI had issued a WATCHCON I alert related to an impending pandemic.

Trump's close associates were reported by *the Times* saying he was "shellshocked," "subdued," and "baffled" when he finally took action in mid-March, influenced mainly by his concern of the negative effect on the economy affecting his re-election chances. Trump's penchant for intolerance of those bearing bad news had been exemplified through a spate of firings after the impeachment hearings. During the COVID-19 crisis, his inspector general at Health and Human Services, Christi Grimm, released a report finding "severe shortages in testing and personal protective gear in hospitals."[167] Shortly after, Grimm was replaced, and she is appealing for being unduly fired as a "whistleblower." Unlike President Truman, who famously said, "The buck stops here," Trump failed to accept responsibility for his tardiness of action—as chronicled by Ian Millhiser of *Vox*,[168] "Trump tells a nation terrified of coronavirus that none of this is his fault." The subtitle of Millhiser's article was, "Trump lied, insulted reporters, and explicitly refused to take responsibility for his own actions."

In the article, Millhiser wrote, "At one point, Trump was asked about the admission of Dr. Anthony Fauci, director of the National Institute of Allergy and Infectious Diseases, that our lag in testing was "a failing." And he was asked if he takes responsibility for this failure."

Trump's response: "I don't take responsibility at all."

Trump's lack of awareness of his shortcomings on both an early understanding of the magnitude of the looming crisis and his need to marshal the federal government to counter the crisis is exemplified by his description of his understanding of the coronavirus.

Hendershot,[169] a current MIT professor, described how Trump views his understanding of the science related to the virus because of his late uncle, an MIT professor. When asked how he knows so much about the coronavirus, Trump responded:

> ... for the vast majority of Americans, the coronavirus poses a "very, very low" risk and that if "we are vigilant ... the virus

will not have a chance against us." And in the course of a visit to the Centers for Disease Control and Prevention last week, Trump attempted to show his mastery of the coronavirus situation by *evoking his uncle*, "a great super genius, Dr. John Trump. I like this stuff. I really get it. People are surprised that I understand it … Maybe I have a natural ability … Maybe I should have been a doctor."

Max Boot, a historian, columnist, and longtime conservative pundit, on April 5, 2020, commenting on Trump's performance regarding the COVID-19 crisis wrote:[170]

Until now, I have generally been reluctant to label Donald Trump the worst president in US history. As a historian, I know how important it is to allow the passage of time to gain a sense of perspective. Some presidents who seemed awful to contemporaries (Harry S. Truman) or simply lackluster (Dwight D. Eisenhower, George H.W. Bush) look much better in retrospect. Others, such as Thomas Jefferson and Woodrow Wilson, don't look as good as they once did …

So I have written, as I did on March 12, that Trump is the worst president in modern times—not of all time. That left open the possibility that James Buchanan, Andrew Johnson, Franklin Pierce, Warren Harding, or some other nonentity would be judged more harshly. But in the past month, we have seen enough to take away the qualifier "in modern times." With his catastrophic mishandling of the coronavirus, Trump has established himself as the worst president in US history.

Trump's failures in creating a federal initiative to counter COVID-19 became fully apparent in an assessment in April 2020—more than three months after the first indication of the oncoming outbreak. Biesecker[171] described an *Associated Press* study showing that the Trump administration squandered nearly two months that could have been used to bolster the federal stockpile of critically needed medical supplies and equipment. Federal agencies waited until mid-March to begin placing bulk orders of N95 respirator masks, ventilators and other equipment needed by frontline health care workers.

The *Baltimore Sun,*[172] in assessing Trump's near-nightly TV appearances, observed:

> ... that frequent presidential chats such as Franklin D. Roosevelt's fireside chats calmed, confident, reassuring, and soothing. They are not remembered as partisan diatribes ... not self-aggrandizing ... Turmoil, conflict, self-love—these are his stock-in-trade ... There is at least one person who has inspired public confidence in the manner of FDR, who has served as the voice of reason, who has been consistent, reliable, honest, and candid. That would be Dr. Anthony S. Fauci.

William Faulk,[173] the editor of *The Week,* who similarly lauded Fauci's daily clean-up of Trump's turmoil and diatribes, described Fauci as having "publicly disagreed with Trump several times without getting fired or shoved into the James Mattis-Rex Tillerson doghouse. For this alone, Fauci deserves a Nobel."

One could dismiss these many critical observations as typical liberal press opinions or, as Trump might describe it, as "fake news." The reality is that these observations can accurately be described as nearly universal, as witnessed by the following spate of articles analyzing Trump's slow reaction to the looming pandemic.

- Ashley Parker,[174] Yasmeen Abutaleb, Lena H. Sun. "Squandered Time—How the Trump administration lost control of the coronavirus crisis," *Washington Post,* March 7, 2020.
- Philip Rucker,[175] Robert Costa, Ashley Parker. "From tweet eruptions to economic steps, Trump struggles for calm amid market meltdown and coronavirus crisis," *Washington Post,* March 9, 2020.
- Dawn Stover, *Mother Jones,* March 14, 2020. 6 Ways the Trump Administration Has Botched Responses to the Coronavirus and Climate Change."

As I described above, my concern centered on how Trump might handle a crisis such as the Cuban Missile Crisis, hopefully by convening his top experts and defining and weighing the pros and cons of strategic actions. As the crisis unfolded, my concern was answered. For example, Trump's daily attendance and active participation in COVID-19 press conferences made no sense given his need to:

- Gather and spend time assessing grand strategy given the myriad of experts that were available to him to evaluate the gravity of the issue concerning infections, deaths, vaccine research, research on test mechanisms, and the shortage of medical supplies/ protective equipment.
- Attend to other significant matters of state and, in particular, related to jobs and projected reopening of the economy.
- Confer with key House and Senate members, local and state government officials, on legislative strategy,

weighing the pros and cons and consequence of bailouts, pump-priming, and future US indebtedness and, in particular, the details of fairness in legislative bailouts.

- Assist developing nations in Latin America and Africa facing their COVID-19 trauma.
- Avoid making contradictory observations devoid of logic and science, e.g., his statement concerning the thought of ingesting disinfectants such as Clorox and the efficacy and safety of taking hydroxychloroquine.

Instead, Trump used the daily press conferences to politic for November 2020, lacing his presentations with references to:

- The best economy ever;
- Obama left the military without ammunition;
- Obama would have taken us to war with North Korea;
- The best stock market ever;
- Contradictory statements in tweets about liberating states including;
  - Michigan, Virginia, and Minnesota implying they could open businesses, etc.; and
- Ingestion of disinfectants such as Clorox as a means to counter the virus.

Trump used the daily press conferences as a "bully pulpit" or "show" without substance. For example, Trump announced that on April 14, he would debut a team full of doctors and business-people to advise him in his rush to *"defibrillate the economy."* [176] Some of the executives named were quoted as saying they were not even aware of being on the list trumpeted by the president.

As stated at the onset, my conclusion, before the election of 2016, bolstered later in hindsight by Rucker and Leonnig's narrative of the Tank meeting, was that Trump could not be trusted to handle grave matters of national import that might arise during his presidency. As shown herein, Trump's equivalent of the Cuban Missile Crisis was the COVID-19 pandemic in which his performance was a monumental failure..

Despite all of Trump's shortcomings, one might be inclined to give him a pass were he to at least have shown some empathy to and for the COVID-19 victims. Frank Bruni captured Trump's lack of empathy[177] in a *New York Times* opinion piece where he contrasts George W. Bush's comments after September 11, and Barack Obama's after the Newtown, Connecticut school shooting with Trump's lack of any semblance of empathy during his many COVID-19 press conferences. Bruni's observations concerning Trump's lack of empathy were described as follows:

> Do you remember the moment when President Trump's bearing and words made clear that he grasped not only the magnitude of this rapidly metastasizing pandemic but also our terror in the face of it? It passed me by, maybe because it never happened … In Trump's predecessors, for all their imperfections, I could sense the beat of a heart and see the glimmer of a soul. In him, I can't, and that fills me with a sorrow and a rage that I quite frankly don't know what to do with.

It is frequently observed that the US is the only developed nation that does not guarantee universal health care to all its citizens. The onset of the coronavirus pandemic has been so overwhelming on our hospitals, health care facilities, doctors, and nurses that even the most conservative legislators have concluded that those needing tests and hospitalization due to the virus should not be denied due to costs or lack of insurance. In fact, the position has been that costs associated with the virus should be part of the various stimulus programs rushed into place by Congress and signed by the president. What is overlooked in this is that so many of our citizens have been in this situation even before the virus.

Many have had to forego medication and/or medical procedures due to an inability to pay and/or lack of insurance. Statistics collected during the COVID-19 pandemic show that minorities and the poor have higher mortality rates from the virus than the population in general—an outcome attributable to pre-existing conditions, which in turn are closely correlated with lack of health care. Alonso-Zaldivar of the *Associated Press* on May 4, 2020,[178] observed that:

> nearly 12 million to 35 million would lose their workplace coverage due to layoffs in the coronavirus shutdown. ... They have more options because of Obamacare law. They are entitled to a special sign-up opportunity or coverage through HealthCare. gov or their state insurance market.

The article quotes Karen Politz of the non-partisan Kaiser Family Foundation as observing that "complications caused by the virus would have been especially radioactive"—essentially meaning that the virus leaves a victim with other ailments considered as a previous existing condition, potentially precluding insurability in the future.

On May 13, 2020, Johnson (*The Hill*) quoted Senator John Cornyn (R-TX) as having "encouraged Americans who have lost health coverage during the coronavirus pandemic, due to losing their jobs, to sign up for Obamacare." Johnson continues, "The senator, who's been in office since 2002, has voted to block, repeal, or defund Obamacare twenty times."

The delays in "social distancing," wearing masks, shutdowns, and development of a meaningful, cohesive national strategy undoubtedly cost many lives as described by a Columbia University study described below. The consequences of the failure to mobilize a quick and timely response to the coronavirus was quantified by a research team of epidemiologists at Columbia University. The team leader, Jeffrey Sharman, reported their finding[179] as follows, "If the United States had begun imposing social distancing measures one week earlier than it did in March, about 36,000 fewer people would have died in the coronavirus outbreak."

One day after *the New York Times* reported the result of the Columbia University study, Trump commented on the study as follows:[180] "Columbia is an institution that's very liberal. I think it is just a political hit job."

Sharman, in an interview after Trump's above comment, suggested that the most critical aspect of his team's analysis was that it should provide a guide for the future—namely the need to identify developing hot spots of coronavirus infections and take early measures tailored to the specific area or region of the projected outbreak. In other words, the models that Sharman and his team used in the study predict that failure to take timely measures as hot spots evolve will lead to countless, needless deaths. Unfortunately, Trump's reaction to the Columbia study and his focus on re-opening the country, without regard to varying regional conditions, is grossly ill-advised and characteristic of his overall failures.

Bret Stephen's conservative credentials include his being a senior editor at the *Wall Street Journal* before he moved to his current editorial position as an opinion columnist at *the New York Times*. In an article[181] with Gail Collins, Stephens provides an insightful summary of Trump's failures in the coronavirus pandemic:

> Trump managed to screw up this crisis in at least six cata-
> strophic ways. He failed to take the COVID threat seriously.
> He presided over a fumbling bureaucratic response. He

embarrassed himself in his press conferences. He tried to throw money at the problem without effectively administering the funds. He demonstrated near-zero empathy with the victims of the disease or their families. And he never really articulated a sensible alternative to the lockdown strategy.

By May 23, 2020, the death toll from COVID-19 in the US approached 100,000. The nation has paused many of its commercial activities, students almost everywhere (and where possible even workers) are working remotely from home. The concepts and reality of "social distancing," "masking," and "quarantine" have become worldwide practices to reduce the spread of the virus. The US Congress has appropriated billions of dollars to assist individuals and businesses who have lost jobs and income. The pharmaceutical industry has aggressive efforts to develop a vaccine(s) to counter the virus. Throughout the crisis, the nation and the world have been beneficiaries of the heroic efforts of medical personnel, food servers, and so many others performing vital services and, in the process, exposing themselves to the virus.

A great national debate has begun on the mechanism and details of restoring a modicum of and path to normalcy in reopening schools, commercial ventures, and manufacturing activities. As discussed herein, the voting process is under debate. Most, unfortunately, the details and pace of the return to normalcy have led to polarization between the right and left and Democrats and Republicans. The nation looks to and needs effective guidance and leadership from its president. On May 23, MSNBC produced a list of churches nationwide that experienced numerous coronavirus deaths of clergy and worshipers after reopening and holding services.

This was the same day that President Trump[182] announced that he would order churches reopened despite the coronavirus pandemic.

7-4. Coronavirus Perils in the Summer of 2020

As of June 13, 2020, numerous states were experiencing their highest caseload of new COVID-19 infections, and the nation was still in shock seeking how best to reopen the economy and, at the same time, avoid major new outbreaks of the virus.

Meanwhile, the president conducted a massive campaign rally in Tulsa, Oklahoma in late June 2020, and due to the expected hazard of spreading the virus, plans were described for all attendees to be notified by words on their rally passes that the GOP would be held blameless should an attendee contract the virus. Mask wearing and social distancing were poorly observed, and the city and the state of Oklahoma paid the price, including the Governor of Oklahoma, who came down with the virus. Herman Cain, a 2012 Republican primary presidential candidate, was photographed at the event with no mask and no social distancing. He acquired the virus and died.

Several state governors seemed to lead the nation in wanting to emphasize "reopening the economy" over more prudent measures suggested by science and medical experts and epidemiologists. This effort quickly led to a spike in COVID-19 cases.

In late July 2020, Rucker of *the Washington Post* described Trump's numerous, recent reversals[183] as related to the then-current coronavirus infestation which was surging out of control:

- Adamant that Congress cut payroll taxes—but backed down;
- Demanded that all of the schools reopen this fall but now allows wiggle room;
- Insisted on filling every seat at the RNC Convention Celebration until he canceled the event; and
- Refused to wear a mask in public and then morphed into a mask evangelist.

As of July 26, 2020, the nation added over one million known cases in fifteen days.[184] By early August, the death toll surpassed 150,000. The grossly ill-advised effort to open the economy at all costs, without a prudently planned, scientifically based, and managed strategy has backfired as witnessed by a letter sent to all governors and the president by 150 Medical Experts.[185] In that letter, the writers urged leaders to shut down the country and start over.

Our friends and allies in Europe have flattened the proverbial curve, and ours is significantly on the rise after many months of national/presidential malfeasance. For this reason, the conclusion is that the Coronavirus was President Trump's equivalent of the Cuban Missile Crisis. He failed us miserably, largely as a result of failing to assemble an early, appropriately staffed brain trust that would have designed a logical plan (for him to implement) to protect the nation's interest rather than his interest in re-election.

Appendix I

Derivation of General Equations for Evaluating the Three Whammy Effects on the Electoral College and the Presidential Election of 2016

Throughout this book, reference is made to the Maximum Whammy Effect and Maximum Whammy Effect Ratio. This ratio is the fundamental mathematical statistic used in this book to analyze how the election of Donald Trump as president was made possible by the Electoral College votes of three states—Michigan, Wisconsin, and Pennsylvania.

This Appendix defines the two variables that constitute this ratio and derives the general equations that are used throughout this book. This includes general equations that apply to each of the three whammies and additional equations that are specific to each whammy. In order, the three sets of equations will be derived for:

1) Whammy No. 1: The Effect of the Comey Letter
2) Whammy No. 2: The Effect of Voter Suppression
3) Whammy No. 3: The Effect of Fake News/Russian Meddling

AI-1 General Definitions:

MWP	Shorthand reference to the three states that tilted the Electoral College, Michigan, Wisconsin, and Pennsylvania.
MWE	The total number of votes switched by a particular whammy.
MWER	The Maximum Whammy Effect Ratio is computed as the ratio of the Maximum Whammy Effect, MWE, divided by the Tilt Margin, TM.

For all three individual whammies, the computation of MWER and TM must differentiate for the apportionment of total votes, MWE, [specified by $(1-z) \times$ MWE] that represent the shift from Clinton to Trump, versus the apportionment $z \times$ MWE that represents the switching from Clinton to third-parties. Note that $z + (1-z) = 1$.

The reason for the partitioning is that votes switched from Clinton to Trump have a doubling effect on the final margin whereas votes switched from Clinton to third- parties have a one to one accounting. The quantity **MTR** represents the Margin of TRump's victory in an MWP state in the 2016 election. This quantity has three unique numbers, one for each MWP state, as shown in Table 2-1 in Chapter 2. In accounting for the effect of the two types of vote switches (and the doubling effect), MWER is thus composed of two components:

$$MWER = MWER2 + MWER1 = MWE\,[(1-z)\,2/MTR + z/MTR] = MWE\,[2-2z+z]/MTR = MWE/MTR/[2(1-z/2)]$$

This leads to the final form of the Tilt Margin TM and MWER:

1) TM = The Tilt Margin = $(MTR)/[2(1-z/2)]$.
2) $MWER = MWE/TM$

With no votes switched to third parties (z = 0), TM would equal MTR/2. The term (1 - z/2) adjusts the formulation to apportion vote switching for vote doubling switches versus those leading to a one to one effect. MWE is computed for a particular whammy to include separate calculations for the Comey Letter, voter suppression, and fake news/Russian meddling.

For adding generality as a function of z to parametric representations, (e.g., Table 4-6 and Figures 4-1, 4-2, and 4-3), this book will represent the quantity:

3) $MWER^* = MWER /(1 - z/2) = MWE/(MTR/2)$

MWER can then be obtained for any value of z by multiplying $MWER^*$ by the quantity (1 - z/2).

Throughout the book and in particular, the parametric analyses used therein, emphasis will be placed on computing the value of MWER because it is a key to understanding the Electoral College phenomenon that occurred. A value of MWER exceeding 1.0 implies that the individual whammy alone was sufficient to tilt the election to Trump. Alternatively, if one whammy were insufficient to tilt the election in a particular MWP state, any sum of two or three individual whammies (represented by MWER's) exceeding 1.0 would similarly lead to the tilting of the election.

AI-2 Definitions and Equations Related to The Comey Letter:

P	The percentage of votes switched due to the Comey Letter. The total votes switched = p x Vtot. Where p = P/100.
NOTE: The polling results represent each candidate's percentage of the total vote. Hence when the polls (between specified dates) show a vote change, the estimate is a projected percentage of the actual number of votes to be cast in the election.	

The conjecture addressed and analyzed, as described in Chapter 2, is that the last-minute Comey Letter, occurring in the last week of the campaign, caused a massive shift of P percentage, in Trump's favor, leading to MWE as follows:

4) $MWE = (P/100)\ Vtot$

The Comey Letter effect is also being examined through statistics on late deciders. In this instance, "late deciders" are voters who essentially made up their minds on who to vote for during the last week before the election, and the conjecture is that they made their decision after being negatively influenced by the Comey Letter. Nate Silver lists relevant polling data on this phenomenon[52].

Definitions for late decider data are the following:

LD	Total percentage of voters who decided late. Here Silver only lists the aggregate average of 12% for the MWP states.
FNET	PT – PC. In a particular MWP state, FNET represents the net percentage (amongst the LD percentage of late deciders) that switched to Trump. PT represents the late deciders who switched to Trump and PC represents the late deciders who switched to Clinton.
	$MWE = Vtot \times [(LD)/100] \times [FNET/100]$

AI-3 Definitions and Equations Related to Voter Suppression:

D	Typical percentage of a targeted group that generally votes for the Democratic candidate
R	Typical percentage of a targeted group that usually votes for a Republican candidate

If the suppression effort is successful in removing a total of Vsup voters from voting (in the targeted group), the gain in votes to the suppressing party is VS = Vsup *(D-R)*.9/100. A nominal 10% adjusts this estimate due to the assumption that a percentage of the otherwise registered voters suppressed, would not have voted anyway in the absence of the suppression. The discussion in Chapter 3 will describe how a statistical strategy called Crosscheck targeted the suppression candidate list and "pulled" a number of votes C as candidates for purging who allegedly were from a candidate list in many states.

Palast[9, 10] obtained data indicating the number of voter registrations "pulled" C (candidates for purging) in each state and that an actual 15.3% of the pulled candidate registrants for purging were actually purged from the voting rolls. The MWE or voter suppression is thus:

5) MWE = .153x C x [(D-R)/100] x .9

AI-4 Definitions and Equations Related to Fake News/ Russian Meddling

The formulas derived in this subsection were used for the calculations in Tables 4-6, 4-7, and 4-8 and Figures 4-1, 4-2, and 4.3. Formulas developed here are borrowed from the analysis of Allcott and Gentzkow.[91, 92, 93]

b and c	The letter "b" attached to a variable refers to "before" and the letter "a" refers to "after," meaning before and after the election with the before period implying a time before voting was affected by switching of votes due to fake news.
c and t	The letters refer to Clinton and Trump, respectively.
Vbc	Number of votes in a specific MWP state for Clinton before any switching of votes.
Vbt	Number of votes in a specific MWP state for Trump before any switching of votes.

Vac	Number of votes in a specific MWP state for Clinton after vote switching.
Vat	Number of votes in a specific MWP state for Trump after vote switching.
SVc	Aggregate or net number of Clinton vote switches (changes) in a particular state caused by fake news (switch away from Clinton). Note: Given the relationships and nominal known values for the respective exposure and persuasion rates, SVc is expected to be positive, meaning votes switched from Clinton to Trump.
Ec	Exposure rate of Clinton voters (units: exposures per voter) to anti-Hillary or pro-Trump fake news.
Et	Exposure rate of Trump voters (units: exposures per voter) to anti-Trump or pro-Clinton fake news.
Pc	Persuasion rate of initial Clinton voters (units: number of switched votes per exposure) likely to switch to Trump because of anti-Clinton or pro-Trump fake news.
Pt	Persuasion rate of initial Trump voters (units: number of switched votes per exposure) likely to switch to Clinton because of anti-Trump or pro-Clinton fake news.

The equation that represents the aggregate of switched votes (due to fake news) away from Clinton to Trump is:

6) $SVc = Vbc \times Ec \times Pc - Vbt \times Et \times Pt$

Because Vbc and Vbt are very close to being equal (see Table 2-1 showing election results), and due to the large variability of SVC caused by the variability of Ec and Pc (compared to the small variability and difference between Vbt and Vbc, we can replace Vbt with Vbc to simplify the computations, which leads to:

7) $SVc = Vbc [Ec \times Pc - Et \times Pt]$

In structuring equations above, voters initially voting for and/or switching from third-party candidates are not included. However, the votes switched "to" a third-party or "other" candidate resulting from fake news, against either Trump or Clinton, will be accounted for later in the model or through the definition of the Tilt Margin as described above. Since actual voting results are available for "after" (Table 2-1) rather than "before" the election, it is also convenient to replace Vbc with Vac. Again, given the large variability of the other variables (and the closeness of the election), this does little damage to the accuracy of the modeling effort. This leads to:

$$8) \quad SVc = Vac \, [Ec \times Pc - Et \times Pt]$$

Note that Clinton loses votes due to fake news if the calculation above leads to SVc being positive above because Ec and Pc are vote swings "away" from Clinton. Data reported before the intelligence findings and listed in AG1 indicate that Ec was three to six times larger than Et. The Congressional hearings on the Russian fake news effort indicated the exposure slant to fake news against Clinton and pro-Trump was even much larger than the three to six factors stated above. *The Wall Street Journal*[100] on November 7, 2017, reported on this slant in various periods on Twitter before election day as varying between 10-to-1, 40-to-1, and 30-to-1 pro-Trump/anti-Clinton. The slant factor A for relating the two exposure rates is represented by:

$$9) \quad Et = Ec/A \text{ with AG2 listing data that suggested } A = 3.75$$
and is much greater for Russian trolling.

Despite the extremely negative news/facts against Trump, those inclined to support him were less likely deterred by anti-Trump, pro-Clinton news, real or fake, and less likely to switch than Clinton supporters, implying that Pc > Pt. Recall, for example, Trump's statement, "I could stand in the middle of Fifth Avenue and shoot somebody, and I wouldn't lose any voters, okay," and Trump's election despite the Access Hollywood video.

We thus similarly employ a slant factor for the persuasion rates:

10) Pt = Pc/B where B is much greater than one since Pc is much greater than Pt.

This leads to:

11) SVc = Vac [Ec Pc - (1/AB) Ec x Pc] = Vac Ec Pc where the nominal value for (1/AB) is very close to zero because of the values of A and B described above. Accordingly, the model reduces to:

12) MWE = SVc = Vac Ec Pc

This is the estimated value for the fake news/Russian meddling Maximum Whammy Effect, obtained by the above derivations and relative value of variables, whose effect will be to provide a means for a global parametric study. Equation (12) represents the estimate of aggregate votes lost by Clinton due to the switching caused by fake news without regard to switching involving third parties. The net effect of third parties (as it affects the Maximum Whammy Effect Ratio) is to reduce the estimate through the definition above by the factor relating the Tilt Margin TM to the Trump margin MTR.

Formulas for the Parametric Study in Chapter 4

The parametric study in Chapter 4 provides two ways in which a wide variation of the Maximum Whammy Effect can be viewed in Tables 4-6, 4-7, and 4-8 and Figures 4-1, 4-2, and 4-3. Table 4-6 lists the value for MWER* = MWER/(1-z/2) for a wide variation of Ec and Pc for each of the three states MWP. MWER* and MWER are related as follows:

13) MWER* = MWER/(1-z/2) = 2Vac Ec Pc /MTR

Table 4-6 provides a parametric listing of MWER* for values of Ec, and Pc using the values in the table heading for Vac and MTR for each of the three states MWP. As noted in this table, the regions for the combined pair of values for which the Maximum Whammy Effect ratio exceeds the value of 1.0 are darkened. Tables 4-7 and 4-8 provide an alternate form of the parametric listing of values predicted by Equation (13). By solving Equation (13) separately for Pc and Ec one obtains:

14) Pc = .5 x MTR x MWER/{Vac x Ec x (-z/2)] {Used for data in Table 4-7)

15) Ec = .5 x MTR x MWER/[[Vac x Pc x (-z/2)] (Used for data in Table 4-8)

The two tables are computed for MWER = 1 [in Equations (14) and (15)], and the table results for both tables can be expanded for any value of MWER by simply multiplying the table values for Pc in Table 4-7 and Ec in Table 4-8 by the desired value of MWER.

Figures 4-1, 4-2, and 4-3 were designed to provide an alternate form of the parametric study. In those graphs, one seeks to define the curves that are formed by expressing Pc (the ordinate) as a function of Ec (the abscissa) with the constraint that the quantity MWER* takes fixed values, in this case, values chosen for MWER* in Equation (13) = .5, 1.0, and 1.5. This was done as follows: An array of fixed values was chosen for Ec varying between .1 to 2.5.

For each of these values of Ec, Pc was calculated from Equation (16) rewritten in the form:

16) $Pc = MWER^* \times .5 \times MTR/(Vac \times Ec)$ for $MWER^* = .5, 1.0,$ and $1.5,$

for each value of Ec in the array, for each of the three MWP states and their associated values of Vac and MTR, as shown in the table headings. This data was then fed to a Microsoft Excel feature, which drew the curves. Based on the rationalization of the values of Ec and Pc, one can then postulate an opinion on the role of fake news and Russian meddling.

Appendix II

Extracts from US Intelligence Assessments of Russian Involvement in Recent US Elections

The extracts below are taken from a document titled, "Assessing Russian Activities and Intentions in Recent US Elections" Intelligence Community Assessment, prepared and published by the Office of the Director of National Intelligence, January 6, 2017.

- Moscow's approach evolved over the course of the campaign based on Russia's understanding of the electoral prospects of the two main candidates. When it appeared to Moscow that Secretary Clinton was likely to win the election, the Russian influence campaign began to focus more on undermining her future presidency.
- We assess with high confidence that Russian military intelligence (General Staff Main Intelligence Directorate of the GRU) used the Guccifer 2.0 persona and DCLeaks.com to release US victim data obtained in cyber operations publicly and in exclusives to media outlets and relayed material to Wikileaks.

Putin Ordered Campaign to Influence US Election

- We also assess Putin and the Russian government aspired to help President-elect Trump's election chances when possible by discrediting Secretary Clinton and publicly contrasting her unfavorably to him. All three agencies agree with this judgment. CIA and FBI have high confidence in this judgment. NSA has moderate confidence.

- Putin most likely wanted to discredit Secretary Clinton because he has publicly blamed her since 2011 for inciting mass protests his regime in late 2011 and early 2012 and because he holds a grudge for comments, he almost certainly saw as disparaging to him in early 2012.

Russian Campaign Was Multifaceted

- Moscow's use of disclosures during the US election was unprecedented. Still, its influence campaign otherwise followed a Russian messaging strategy that blends covert intelligence operations—such as cyber activity—with overt efforts by Russian government agencies, state-funded media, third-party intermediaries. It paid social media users or "trolls."

Public Disclosures of Russian Collected Data

- We assess with high confidence that the GRU used the Guccifer 2.0 persona, DCLeaks.com, and Wikileaks to release US victim data obtained in cyber operations publicly and exclusives to media outlets.

- We assess with high confidence that the GRU relayed material it acquired from the DNC and senior Democratic officials to Wikileaks. Moscow most likely chose Wikileaks because of its self-proclaimed reputation for authenticity. Disclosures through Wikileaks did not contain any evident forgeries.

Russia Today (RT) and Russian Propaganda Efforts

- The Kremlin's principal international propaganda outlet RT (formerly Russia Today), has actively corroborated with Wikileaks. RT's editor-in-chief visited Wikileaks founder Julian Assange at the Ecuadorian Embassy in London in August 2013, where they discussed renewing his broadcast contract with RT, according to Russian and Western media. Russian media subsequently announced that RT had become "the only Russian media company" to partner with Wikileaks and had received access to "new leaks of secret information." RT routinely gives Assange sympathetic coverage and provides him a platform to denounce the United States.

- State-owned Russian media made increasingly favorable comments about President-elect Trump as the 2016 US general and primary election campaigns progressed while consistently offering negative coverage of Secretary Clinton.

- On August 6, RT published an English-language video called "Julian Assange Special: Do Wikileaks Have the Email That'll Put Clinton in Prison?" and an exclusive interview with Assange titled "Clinton and ISIS Funded by the Same Money." RT's most popular video on Secretary Clinton, "How 100% of the Clinton's Charity Went to Themselves," had more than nine million views on social media platforms. RT's most popular English language video about the president-elect "Trump Will Not be Permitted to Win," featured Assange and had 2.2 million views.

- Russia used trolls as well as RT as part of the influence efforts to denigrate Secretary Clinton. This effort amplified stories on scandals about Secretary Clinton and the role of Wikileaks in the election campaign.

- A journalist who is a leading expert on the Internet Research Agency claimed that some social media accounts that appear to be tied to Russia's professional trolls—because they previously were devoted to supporting Russian actions in Ukraine-started to advocate for President-elect Trump as early as December 2015.

RT Focuses on Social Media, Building Audience

- According to RT management, RT's website receives at least 500,000 unique viewers every day. Since its inception in 2005, RT videos received more than 800 million views on YouTube (one million views per day), which is the highest among news outlets (see graphics for comparison with other news channels) (AKT October 4).

- RT states on its website that it can reach more than 550 million people worldwide and 85 million people in the United States: however, it does not publicize its actual US audience numbers (RT, December 10).

Formal Disassociation from Kremlin Facilitates RT US Messaging

- RT America formally disassociates itself from the Russian government by using a Moscow-based autonomous nonprofit organization to finance its US operations. According to RT's leadership, this structure was set up to avoid the Foreign Agents Registration Act and to facilitate licensing abroad.

Appendix III

Headlines are Wrong—Polls Show That Americans Support Obamacare

This paper is on my website and was written in 2013 shortly after the Republicans shut down the government in protest against the Affordable Care Act. It has been edited for consistency with the book's contents. www.complexpolitics.wordpress.com

●　●　●　●　●

I was eighteen years old when my mother died at the age of forty-eight of congestive heart failure. When I was twenty-two, my father died at the age of fifty-three from a heart attack. What we had in common was poverty, lack of a family doctor, no preventative health care, or health insurance, nor the means to pay for any major medical emergency.

Admittedly few people had insurance in those days, circa 1958-1962. In later years as I went through four significant illnesses and three major surgeries, my family and I were fortunate to have both excellent health insurance and Medicare, great doctors, and the benefit of the great strides in medical science. This lifetime perspective, contrasting my parents' early deaths with my own extended longevity, influences my thinking, as I, like most Americans, watch the national debate on the Affordable Care Act (ACA), or Obamacare, and the defunding of government as a means to repeal the ACA.

The debate grapples with the reality that today, like my parents then, we find tens of millions of Americans without health insurance nor the means to avail themselves of life-saving medical care and technology.

As an interested observer of a variety of fact and opinion on matters of national and international import, in print, broadcast media and the internet, I have been struck with the need to express an opinion on the national debate on the ACA and the Republican effort to delay or defund the ACA as a condition for continuing government operations. I interpret a major part of the Conservative argument against the ACA to be that the public is against the health initiative, and the press headlines support this contention. I see it differently as I process the vast collection of information and opinion on the ACA.

Counter to these headlines, I base my view largely on the results of two major, frequently cited polls that asked a cross-section of Americans, Republicans, Democrats, and Independents, whether they support or oppose various aspects of health care policy that are components of the ACA. Rather than focus on the single question of being for or against the ACA as a whole, for reasons I will describe, I view the aggregate of responses to the component questions as being far more meaningful. Examination of the polling results in the table below one finds robust support for twelve of the thirteen components of the ACA, the only component not gaining favor is the so-called individual mandate, that all citizens obtain health care. I also note in the table the overall result against the ACA legislation as a whole—the typical result that generally makes the headlines.

176

As I write this, I have the added benefit of a recent article from *The New York Times* on October 5, 2013, titled "A Federal Budget Crisis Months in the Planning." The article describes how a coalition of conservative activists met shortly after President Obama's second inauguration and laid out a grand strategy to repeal Mr. Obama's health care law. *The Times* listed various groups in the coalition that arose from this meeting [hereafter referred to as the Kill Obamacare Coalition (KOC)] to include the Heritage Foundation, the Club for Growth, Freedom Works, Tea Party Patriots, and Freedom Partners Chamber of Commerce link to the Koch Brothers, Charles, and David.

In recent days we have seen how the KOC grand strategy has led to the government shutdown in an attempt to defund and/or delay or repeal the ACA. *The Times* article states, "With polls showing Americans deeply divided over the law, conservatives believe that the public is behind them." The article goes on to quote Michelle Bachman, congresswoman from Minnesota, founder of the House Tea Party Caucus, on the eve of the government shutdown, "This is exactly what the public wants."

With the individual mandate being the only ACA component disfavored by the public, it is revealing to analyze the juxtaposition of the Heritage Foundation, a key member of KOC, being the original dominant proponent of the individual mandate, with its current role leading the crusade against the ACA, with a special focus opposing the individual mandate.

KOC is prominently represented in the coalition by the group called Heritage Action for America, the political arm of the Heritage Foundation headed by Michael Needham. Needham's role in KOC was extensively chronicled in the *Wall Street Journal* on October 12 in an article by Stephen Moore of the WSJ staff. The Heritage Foundation itself is now headed by former Republican US Senator Jim DeMint from South Carolina who has turned the Foundation into one of the most active opponents of Obamacare.

For perspective on this turnaround, we turn to the Heritage Foundation paper, Lecture #218, October 1, 1989, titled, "Assuring Affordable Care for All Americans." The author of the paper is Stuart M. Butler, then director of domestic policy studies at the Heritage Foundation. In the article, Butler states: "As many as 37 million Americans lack adequate insurance against health care cost, and many others who have insurance still dread the financial impact of a serious disease." Toward a plan to overcome this national problem, Butler proposed two key concepts:

1) Direct and indirect government assistance should be concentrated on those who need it most. Help should be provided to those who cannot afford protection.
2) Mandate all households to obtain adequate insurance.

In rationalizing the proposed mandate, Butler stated,

Thus we find many individuals and families, particularly among the young, who decide to use their income for other objectives than health care insurance, even though they have the means to obtain insurance without cutting back on other necessities...They are playing Russian roulette with their continued good health. The household mandate assumes that it is the family that carries the first responsibility...there is an implicit contract between households and society based on the notion that health insurance is not like other forms of insurance. If a young man wrecks his Porsche and has not had the foresight to obtain insurance, we may commiserate, but society feels no obligation to repair his car. But health care is different. If a man is struck down by a heart attack in the street, Americans will care for him whether or not he has insurance. If we find that he has spent his money on other things rather than insurance, we may be angry, but we will not deny him services—even if it means more prudent citizens end up paying the tab.

One must note that this latter concept (of not denying medical service in emergencies) was ingrained in 1986 legislation, the Emergency Medical Treatment and Active Labor Act (EMTALA) and was co-sponsored by Republican Senator Robert Dole and Democratic Congressman Pete Stark, passed by a Democratic House and Republican Senate, and signed by Republican President Ronald Reagan. The act mandates that any hospital participating in Medicare (or receiving funds from the Department of Health and Human Services) must provide emergency services to anyone, including illegal immigrants, whether they can pay or not.

Accordingly, very few hospitals are exempt from this EMTALA requirement. There is considerable evidence that EMTALA (due to so-called free riders) has led to cost-shifting (or hidden tax) primarily through higher rates for insured individuals with hospitalization insurance. Harbage and Nichols (2006), of the New America Foundation, in a paper titled "The Hidden Costs All Californians Pay in Our Fragmented Health Care System" estimate that this cost-shifting due to free riders "amounted to $455 per individual or $1,186 per family in California each year."

Professor Matt Harman, in a web article titled "EMTALA and the Costs of Providing Health Care to the Uninsured," citing data from the American Medical Association on unpaid care, estimates a 13% added cost to insurance premiums in Texas versus a national average of 8%. The hidden tax posed by EMTALA could thus be viewed as the basis for Butler's ringing endorsement of the individual mandate. Governor Romney incorporated the individual mandate in Massachusetts Romneycare to overcome the costs of EMTALA and attributed the idea to former House Speaker Newt Gingrich, who, in turn, got the idea from Butler and the Heritage Foundation.

In following the KOC campaign against Obamacare by the coalition described by *the New York Times*, it is a fact that one of the features of the ACA most railed against is the individual mandate —most ironically the feature given legs by the Heritage Foundation as described above. In contrast to the concepts of young free-riders being a financial drag on emergency rooms, described so graphically by Butler in the Heritage paper, KOC through Freedom Works and Jim Demint's National Town Halls, have introduced the concept that young, healthy workers will unjustly be forced to subsidize their sicker elders, thus treating young people unfairly. Butler, who remains at Heritage as the current director for policy innovation, states his reversal and now opposition to the individual mandate as arising from the following:

a) It is unconstitutional;
b) It forces people to buy expensive comprehensive coverage rather than catastrophic coverage; and
c) It forces individuals to buy insurance without a requirement. Of course, the Supreme Court has since ruled the ACA is constitutional.

One of the most extensive analyses of the individual mandate is a paper by Eibner and Price of the Rand Corporation titled "The Effect of the Affordable Care Act on Enrollment and Premiums, with and Without the individual mandate." They address the notion of unjust treatment of young, healthy workers by observing that "because younger individuals are more likely to be low-income, the ACA subsidy schedule is disproportionately generous to younger, lower-cost people." The provision that individuals under age twenty-six can remain on their parent's insurance further mitigates any perceived unfairness.

The ACA's provisions for levels of insurance labeled bronze, silver, gold, and platinum, with the bronze plan being limited coverage, along with the subsidies and insurance on parent's plan through age twenty-six, largely mitigates any concern for expensive comprehensive coverage cited by Butler as a basis for his reversal of opinion on the individual mandate.

Matt Miller, in *the Washington Post,* August 21, 2013, in an article titled, "The GOP's Obamacare Youth Hoax" observes that 20 million youth between the ages of nineteen and thirty-four get health insurance through their employer and effectively pay the same rate as their elders for the same insurance and have done so for decades without a peep from anyone about this socialistic unfairness. Butler's original anecdote, quoted above about the Porsche owners wreck versus the man struck down on the street by a heart attack, remains a solid argument why mandated insurance should be a requirement. Others have opposed the mandate because it is socialistic. Yes, it is socialistic, but so is the mandate imposed by EMTALA.

Concerning costs under the ACA Exchange Policies, one of the key findings of the Eibner-Price Rand study is the conclusion, "With our methods, we find a 9.3% increase in the average premium per covered life when the mandate is repealed" primarily "due to a change in the composition of enrollees." Their overall conclusion states, "Our analysis demonstrates that the individual mandate is important to achieving the goal of near-universal coverage for all Americans."

Jonathon Gruber, a professor of economics at the Massachusetts Institute of Technology, was a principal architect of the Romney Massachusetts health reform insurance legislation and an advisor to Democrats and the Obama administration during the build of the Affordable Care Act. Gruber has been quoted as comparing Obamacare with Romneycare by saying, "the two were the "same (expletive deleted) bill." In an August 2013 Massachusetts poll conducted by the Massachusetts Medical Society Physicians Group and reported on by Healthwatch, 84% expressed satisfaction with their health care. In a 2008 paper in the Journal of Economic Literature, titled, "Covering the Uninsured in the United States," Gruber introduces a metric of new government spending per new insurance enrollee called "bang for the buck." His modeling indicates that with the mandate, the total government cost per enrollee is $3,659, and without the mandate, the cost is $7,468—essentially a factor of two. The huge difference is due to the fact that government spending will be roughly the same, with or without the mandate, but 12.5 million fewer people will gain coverage without the mandate.

The KOC effort to kill Obamacare with a focus on this alleged unprecedented unfairness is an incredible irony. It is undoubtedly the reason that the individual mandate is the one component of the ACA that is not supported by a majority of those polled. *The Times* article indicates that the Koch brothers, through Freedom Partners Chamber of Commerce, have disbursed more than $200 million in the KOC effort. The campaign has featured young people enticed into demonstrations featured by "Burn Your Obamacare Draft Card" rallies, inferring that the individual mandate is unfair to youth—comparing it to the military draft.

As the effort to kill Obamacare (KOC) proceeds, along with the government remaining shut down along with the threat of default due to a **failure to** lift the debt ceiling, this writer is reminded of a recent cartoon. An elephant is standing beside an oncoming train that is labeled "Obamacare." A portion of the track has been removed in the train's path, and the reader gets the image of the oft-repeated claim that Obamacare is headed for a train wreck. However, the frame with the elephant shows the elephant with a crowbar and other tools by which the missing segment of the track has been removed—assuring the impending train wreck. The KOC effort is determined to create an Obamacare train wreck.

My plea to KOC Conservatives is, "Please put away your crowbars." Your misguided efforts are leading us to a national train wreck.

Polling Results on the Key Features of ACA Amongst Democrats, Republicans, and Independents		
	Reuters/Ipsos Poll June 2012	Kaiser Health Tracking Poll March 2013
Dependents Coverage to Age 26	63% For	76% For
Ban on Denying Coverage for Pre-existing Conditions	82% For	Not Asked
Disallow Policy Cancellation After Sickness/Guaranteed Issue	86% For	66% For
Creation of Health Insurance Exchanges	80% For	89% For
Ban on Lifetime Caps	80% For	Not Asked
Regulations to Insure Comparable Coverage	68% For	Not Asked
Mandating companies with 50 or more employees to provide coverage	73% For	57% For
Subsidies to Help the Poor	75% For	76% For
Expanding Medicaid for Family Incomes Under $35,000	64% For	71% For
Tax Credits For Small Businesses Providing Insurance Coverage	Not Asked	88% For

Closing Medicare Donut Hole	Not Asked	81% For
Increase Medicare Payroll Tax for Upper Incomes	60% For	Not Asked
Mandate All Citizens Obtain Health Coverage*	59% Against	60% Against
Support for the Overall Legislation*	55 % Against, 45% For	40% Against, 37% For, No opinion 23%

*A May 27, 2013, CNN/ORC poll found 54% opposed to Obamacare and 43% in support. However, of those opposed, 16% said they oppose the law because it isn't liberal enough.

Appendix IV

Trump: the Muslim Ban and the Lessons of History—The Historical Clash Between Security and Human Rights

This article was posted on the author's web site on February 1, 2017, at www.complexpolitics.wordpress.com. It has been edited for consistency with the book's contents.

The current presidential directive, generally referred to as extreme vetting and/or the Muslim ban, is examined in the context of its rationale being that of security. Its opponents suggest it was poorly planned and executed and, in its implementation, has the likelihood of major human rights violations and being unconstitutional. This paper suggests that the lessons of history were ignored and how those lessons might have provided caution and guidance if the president was an avid student of history.

Four examples of how concerns for security in the US and North America led to extreme measures which in the historical aftermath were universally decried by historians and citizenry in general because of their catastrophic impact on human rights.

• • • • •

Our new president has been quoted as receiving much of his information from television. The consensus understanding is that, unlike many of his predecessors in the presidency, he is poorly read on history. A famous quote from the philosopher George Santayana is, "Those who fail to learn from history are doomed to repeat it." This admonition could well apply to our new president as the US faces protests internally and all over the world regarding what is interpreted as a ban on Muslims entering the US. While the president disagrees that his recent executive order is a Muslim ban, former New York mayor Rudy Giuliani is quoted as saying that Trump tasked him to charter a commission to determine how a Muslim ban could be legally implemented. This has been widely viewed as putting a sheen of acceptance on a policy that otherwise has been interpreted, both in the US and overseas, as a Muslim ban. The president's executive order is designed as a security measure; the opposition cites it as being unconstitutional and, in essence, a violation of human rights.

Similar actions in our history provide the history lessons that our president might have been influenced by, were he an avid reader. Current day Americans decry the roundup of the ethnic Japanese and their forced internment in WWII. They also decry the turn away of the shipload of 900 European Jews in 1939, which led to the eventual death of 264 of those turned away in the Holocaust. One should also mention the plight of the Native Americans in the Trail of Tears as 20,000 were illegally marched westward at gunpoint from their ancestral homes in Georgia, with one fourth dying in the journey and countless others dying later from the upheaval. This historical event, like the current one, was an example of a clash between presidential action and the courts.

The often expressed sentiment that "we are all immigrants" particularly comes to my mind as I think of the plight of those who have been and will be affected by the president's edict on visa

186

restrictions so as provide a period for developing a new posture of "extreme vetting." Of note in the national debate is the fact that the president has not shared with us the current details in the vetting process, the alleged deficiencies, how they may be improved, and instances where current vetting has led to the ills he seeks to correct and how a legal, humane, plan could be thoughtfully designed and legally be implemented. It should be noted that Glenn Kessler, *Washington Post* fact checker, on January 30, found that the number of personnel affected by the visa restrictions is not 109, as stated by President Trump, but closer to 90,000.

Perhaps the president could be excused from knowing the history lesson I want to describe in this piece because it has been described as the "lost chapter in American history." Before Jamestown, before Plymouth Rock, in 1603, my Acadian ancestors fled poverty and hopelessness in France and settled in northern Maine and later the vicinity of the Canadian Bay of Fundy, and named it Acadia, which is now Nova Scotia (New Scotland). These immigrants tamed the marshlands, farmed, fished, hunted, befriended, and some intermarried with the Native American Micmacs. They prospered despite becoming pawns between the two great powers France and England. Hegemony over these Acadian immigrants exchanged hands ten times between 1604 and 1710. In times of British occupation, the Acadians were never in revolt; there were no guerilla bands of Acadians assassinating their British occupiers despite their having to supply the British with food and fuel, no say in their governance and the constant entreaties from the French stronghold in Quebec urging them to revolt.

From 1704 to 1755, the British occupied Acadia for the tenth time. In 1755, tensions ran high between France and England (similar to our present concerns about terrorism), in a time that was a prelude to the French and Indian War. Despite the 150 years of peaceful history of the Acadians, and their subservience to their intermittent English masters, some, in particular British Governor Lawrence, and Massachusetts colonial Governor Shirley, viewed the Acadians as threats should war come. Like today, the issue became one of security—the British fear that Acadians would assist the French in the looming war. Like Trump today, viewing Muslims as threats, Lawrence overreacted (admittedly much more severely) and came up with a plan to remove all Acadians from their ancestral home. The program becomes known in history as "le Grand Derangement" (the great upheaval). Ships and militia are equipped by Governor Shirley in Massachusetts, augmented by British troops, forces go ashore in Acadia, round up inhabitants, burn their homes, load them aboard ships ill-equipped for the voyage and, in the words of a book title by the Acadian historian, Carl Brasseau, are "Scattered to the Wind."

They are deposited in small groups throughout the New England colonies. Like the Trump actions of this week, the expulsion is poorly planned, the ships are ill-equipped to handle their cargo, Virginia and South Carolina refuse to accept the refugees, they sit for weeks aboard overcrowded ships, little food, poor sanitation, and sickness. They are eventually sent to prisons in England. Three ships sank in various journeys losing all aboard (except the crews).

Years later, at war's end, the Acadian survivors seek to find new homes, some wind up in the tropics of St. Domingue, and others as far as the Falkland Island. Many go to Louisiana. The Yale historian John Mack Faragher describes how, in July 1755, Acadians numbered some eighteen thousand persons. Over the next eight years after the deportation, an estimated ten thousand exiles lost their lives mostly from shock, exhaustion, dehydration, starvation, and disease. Ninety years later, Longfellow kept their story alive in his book-length poem *Evangeline*.

My Breaux ancestors were dumped into southern Maryland and survived due to the good graces of the nearby Catholic St. Thomas Manor. My LeBlanc great grandparents, Rene LeBlanc and Anne Theriot, escaped deportation by fleeing into the Canadian woods in Miramichi, surviving for a time but always on the move seeking to avoid the ravages of British raids on their makeshift encampments and like many others eventually dying of exposure and starvation. My surviving Breaux and Le Blanc ancestors eventually migrated to Louisiana, then under Spanish rule. Most ironically, several joined the Acadian militia under the Spanish governor Galvez and helped to expel the British from the lower Mississippi during their former colonial adversaries War for Independence. After the Louisiana Purchase, they became U. S. citizens. For their service, my children and I qualify as "Sons and Daughters of the American Revolution."

Yes, we are all immigrants. Our histories vary, but the common theme is that America, in the words of de Tocqueville, "is a beacon of hope." As our president, his advisors, and our Congress seek to protect us from terrorism and debate the details, wisdom, and legality of President Trumps' recent edict, I am reminded of the dialogue in the British Parliament after the time of the Acadian expulsion.

The famed parliamentarian, Edmund Burke, in 1780, in decrying the historical actions of his government, stated, "It seems our nation had more skill and ability in destroying rather than settling a colony. In the last war, we did in my opinion, most inhumanely, and upon pretenses that in the eye of an honest man are not worth a farthing, root out these poor, innocent, deserving people whom our utter inability to govern, or to reconcile, gave us no right to extirpate."

In 1992, after years of effort by Louisiana attorney Warren Perrin, including numerous presentations to international human rights conferences, Queen Elizabeth of England apologized for the British actions in the deportation of the Acadians.

Historically, we regret the deportation of the Acadians, the internment of the Japanese, the expulsion and forced march of the Cherokee, the turn away of the shipboard Jews. Today we are in a national discussion, and admittedly the issue seems less extreme than the historical instances cited herein. Still, nevertheless, we are in a position to learn the lessons of that history.

Today, like the four historical examples cited, an action has been predicated on concern for security and has severe implications on legality and human rights. Let us join together and urge our national government to heed these lessons of history as they contemplate a just and humane course of legislation and action related to vetting and acceptance of refugees. Let us hope that the course of action we take leads us not to an Edmund Burke of the future having to decry our historical action.

Epilogue

The research and writing that led to Chapter 3 dealing with voter suppression and Chapter 4 dealing with fake news/ Russian involvement have provided insights that are relevant to voting in the 2020 election.

Voter suppression is rampant through numerous measures described in this book. One can expect efforts to continue using those measures. In the summer of 2020, planning to vote by mail was most important in the coming presidential election because of the need to maintain "social distancing" because of COVID-19. The national experience at polling places in recent elections (pre-COVID-19) is rife with examples of long lines of voters, which in many instances discourage people from voting. Additionally, COVID-19 has already (and will further) lead to fewer volunteers to man the voting stations. President Trump has begun an almost daily crusade of misinformation against the concept of mail-in-balloting. The result is that the nation will be ill prepared due to the lack of funding, planning, and preparation for mail-in balloting.

Additionally, indication is that Trump has taken steps, implemented by his newly appointed postmaster czar, to effectively "slow down the mail." This factor, plus the lack of preparation, could result in Trump's prediction of mail fraud and delays becoming a self-fulfilling prophecy.

Both domestic and Russian fake news is characterized by exposure rate and persuasion rate, as described herein. It should be noted that the numbers (for these two variables) reported herein (and their implication) are averages across a range determined by 248 million voters and 370 million US adults. However, the election of 2016 was determined by three so-called battleground states—Michigan, Wisconsin, and Pennsylvania. Hereafter, anyone schooled in and devising election strategy will likely focus on the Electoral College and states that are most amenable to be carried by their candidate. Accordingly, one envisions a strategy devoted to designing fake news that targets sub-populations of voters with a pitch that is cleverly designed toward well known "sore points" that are unique to the sub-population. The two reports[84,85] to the Senate, the Oxford University and New Knowledge Study, highlighted the fact that such a strategy is/was in place in 2016. One can thus expect this kind of strategy to be the norm hereafter, but greatly accelerated, given the success as documented by this book. If such strategies are employed, one can expect larger values of both exposure and persuasion rates (and a greater effect) than that analyzed herein. Such a tactic poses a grave threat to our democracy and as a result preventive measures must be undertaken. Unfortunately, as the article by Miller et al[60] suggests "Trump pursues Putin and leaves a Russian threat unchecked."

Acknowledgments

To my wonderful wife, Priscilla: thank you for encouraging me from idea to published book.

To my beloved children, Mary Toler, Susie Breaux McShea, and Mark Breaux: without you, this book would still be on my computer.

To my editor, Deborah Kevin: thank you for the care you put into making this book a reality.

About the Author

Harold J. Breaux, a Louisiana native, enjoyed a fifty-year career at the Aberdeen Proving Ground Ballistic Research Laboratory (BRL) and Army Research Laboratory (ARL) in Maryland. He authored over forty government publications and twelve refereed journal articles. In 2010, the ARL named its fastest and newest supercomputer the "Harold" in honor of his professional contributions. In 2012, the Harford County Cultural Arts Board named Breaux a "Harford Living Treasure" for his lifetime contributions to the county. This is his first book.

References

Introduction

1   Wolff, Michael. *Fire and Fury: Inside the Trump White House.* Henry Holt and Company, 2018.

2   Olsen, Matthew, and Benjamin Haas. "The Electoral College Is A National Security Threat: The Founding Fathers Never Anticipated the Rise of Facebook and Fake News." Conservative Daily Post, September 21, 2017. https://conservativedailypost.com/the-electoral-college-is-a-national-security-threat-liberal-politico-now-pushing-for-collapse/.

3   Alexander, Peter. "Trump's Electoral College Win Was Not the Biggest Since Reagan." *NBC News,* February 16, 2017. https://www.nbcnews.com/politics/donald-trump/trump-s-electoral-college-win-was-not-biggest-reagan-n722016.

4   Davis, Lanny J. *The Unmaking of the President 2016: How FBI Director James Comey Cost Hillary Clinton the Presidency.* New York: Scribner, 2018.

5   Nance, Malcolm, *The Plot to Hack America: How Putin's Cyberspies and WikiLeaks Tried to Steal the 2016 Election.* Skyhorse Publishing, 2016.

6   Nance, Malcolm, *The Plot to Betray America: How Team Trump Embraced our Enemies, Compromised Our Security, and How We Can Fix It.* New York: Hachette Books, 2019.

7   Jamieson, Kathleen Hall. *Cyberwar: How Russian Hackers and Trolls Helped Elect a President: What We Don't, Can't, and Do Know.* New York, NY: Oxford University Press, 2018.

8   Meyer, Jane. "How Russia Helped Swing the Election for Trump." *New Yorker,* September 24, 2018.

9   Palast, Greg, and Greg Palast. "The GOP's Stealth War Against Voters." *Rolling Stone,* August 24, 2016.

10 Palast, Greg. "The Election Was Stolen – Here's How." Rise Up Times, November 14, 2016. https://riseuptimes.org/2016/11/12/greg-palast-the-election-was-stolen-heres-how/.

11 deBuys, William. "How to Hijack an Election." Vox Populi, January 21, 2017. https://voxpopulisphere.com/2017/01/20/william-debuys-how-to-hijack-an-election/.

12 Abadi, Mark. "Donald Trump Blasted the Electoral College in 2012, Before It Gave Him the Presidency." Business Insider, November 2016. http://www.businessinsider.com/donald-trump-electoral-college-popular-vote-2016-11.

13 Greenwood, Max. "Exclusive: Trump Campaign Training Army of Volunteers in 2020 States." The Hill, July 19, 2019. https://thehill.com/homenews/campaign/453911-trump-campaign-rnc-training-army-of-volunteers-in-key

Chapter 1

14 Johnston, David Cay. The Making of Donald Trump. Melville House, 2016.

15 Zirin, James D. Plaintiff in Chief: A Portrait of Donald Trump in 3500 Lawsuits. All Print Books, 2019.

16 Penzenstadler, Nick, and Susan Page. "Exclusive: Trump's 3500 Lawsuits Unprecedented for a Presidential Nominee." USA Today, June 1, 2019. https://www.usatoday.com/story/news/politics/elections/2016/06/01/donald-trump-lawsuits-legal-battles/84995854/.

17 The Point: The Secret Why Trump Won't Release His Taxes. CNN. Cable News Network, 2019. https://www.cnn.com/videos/tv/2019/04/09/cnngo-the-point-secret-why-trump-wont-release-his-taxes-cillizza.cnn.

18 Donald Trump Calls Father's $1 Million Loan 'Small.' Bing, 2015. https://www.bing.com/videos/search?q=Trump one million dollar loan.

19 Matthews, Dylan. "Donald Trump Isn't Rich Because He's a Great Investor. He's Rich Because His Dad Was Rich." Vox, March 30, 2016. https://www.vox.com/2015/9/2/9248963/donald-trump-index-fund.

20 Fisher, Marc, and Will Hobson. "Donald Trump Masqueraded as Publicist to Brag About Himself." Washington Post, May 13, 2016. https://www.washingtonpost.com/politics/donald-trump-alter-ego-barron/2016/05/12/02ac99ec-16fe-11e6-aa55-670cabef46e0_story.html.

21   Greenberg, Jonathan. "Trump Lied to Me About His Wealth to Get onto the Forbes 400. Here Are the Tapes." *Washington Post*, April 20, 2018. https://www.washingtonpost.com/outlook/trump-lied-to-me-about-his -wealth-to-get-onto-the-forbes-400-here-are-the-tapes/2018/04/20/ ac762b08-4287-11e8-856.

22   D'Antonio, Michael. "Donald Trump's Long Strange History of Using Fake Names." *Fortune*, February 2, 2016. https://fortune.com/2016/05/18/ donald-trump-fake-names/.

23   Buettner, Russ, Susanne Craig, and David Barstow. "11 Takeaways from *the Times* Investigation into Trump's Wealth." *New York Times*, October 2, 2018. https://www.nytimes.com/2018/10/02/us/politics/donald-trump-wealth -fred-trump.html.

24   Rosenthal, Max J. "The Trump Files: The Shady Way Fred Trump Tried to Save His Son's Casino." *Mother Jones*, September 26, 2016. https://www.motherjones.com/politics/2016/09/trump-files-fred-trump -funneled-cash-donald-using-casino-chips/.

25   NPR Staff. "Decades-Old Housing Discrimination Case Plagues Donald Trump." *NPR*, September 30, 2016. https://www.npr.org/2016/09/29/495955920/donald-trump-plagued-by -decades-old-housing-discrimination-case.

26   Kranish, Michael, and Robert O'Harrow. "Inside the Government's Racial Bias Case against Donald Trump's Company, and How He Fought It." *Washington Post*, January 23, 2016. https://www.washingtonpost.com/politics/inside-the-governments-racial -bias-case-against-donald-trumps-company-and-how-he-fought-it/2016/01/ 23/fb90163e-bfbe-11e5-b.

27   Pearl, Mike. All the Evidence We Could Find About Fred Trump's Alleged Involvement with the KKK, March 10, 2016. https://www.vice.com/en_uk/ article/mvke38/all-the-evidence-we-could-find-about-fred-trumps-alleged -involvement-with-the-kkk.

28   Calabrese, Massimo. "What Donald Trump Knew About Undocumented Workers at His Signature Tower." *The Muslim Times*, August 25, 2016. https://themuslimtimes.info/2016/08/25/what-donald-trump-knew-about -undocumented-workers-at-his-signature-tower/.

29   Fahrenthold, David. "Trump Used $258,000 From His Charity to Settle Legal Problems." *Washington Post*, September 20, 2016. https://www.washingtonpost.com/politics/trump-used-258000-from-his -charity-to-settle-legal-problems/2016/09/20/adc88f9c-7d11-11e6-ac8e -cf8e0dd91dc7_stor.

30   Fahrenthold, David. "New York Files Civil Suit against President Trump, Alleging His Charity Engaged in 'Illegal Conduct'." *The Washington Post*, June 14, 2018. https://www.washingtonpost.com/politics/new-york-files-suit-against -president-trump-alleging-his-charity-engaged-in-illegal-conduct/2018/06/14/ c3cbf71e-6fc9-11e8-bd50-b80389a4e569_story.html.

31   Blitzer, Ronn. "Trump Ordered to Pay $2M in Trump Foundation Settlement, Admits Misuse of Funds." *Fox News*, November 8, 2019. https://www.foxnews.com/politics/potus-to-pay-2-million-admits-misuse-of -trump-foundation-funds-in-settlement-with-ny-ag.

32   Breuninger, Kevin, and Dan Mangan. "Trump Ordered to Pay $2 Million to Settle Suit Claiming Trump Foundation Misused Funds to Benefit Campaign." *CNBC*, November 8, 2019. https://www.cnbc.com/2019/11/07/ trump-ordered-to-pay-2-million-to-settle-trump-foundation-suit.html.

33   McMillan, Keith. "Trump Received 'Bone Spurs' Diagnosis as a 'Favor,' Doctor's Daughters Allege." *The Washington Post*, December 26, 2018. https://www.washingtonpost.com/politics/2018/12/26/trump-received -bone-spurs-diagnosis-favor-doctors-daughters-allege/.

34   Marquina, Sierra. "Donald Trump Calls Sleeping Around His 'Personal Vietnam'." *Us Weekly*, February 9, 2018. https://www.usmagazine.com/celebrity-news/news/donald-trump-calls -sleeping-around-as-his-personal-vietnam-w432176/.

35   Cassidy, John, Adam Gopnik, and Vauhini Vara. "Trump University: It's Worse Than You Think." *The New Yorker*, June 2, 2016. https://www.newyorker.com/news/john-cassidy/trump-university-its -worse-than-you-think.

36   Zarya, Valentina. "No One Knows What Donald Trump Did at Wharton." *Fortune*, August 14, 2015. https://fortune.com/2015/08/14/ donald-trump-wharton/.

37   Fouhy, Beth. "Trump: Obama a 'Terrible Student' Not Good Enough for Harvard." *NBC New York*, April 26, 2011. https://www.nbcnewyork.com/news/local/Trump-Obama-Wasnt-Good -Enough-to-Get-into-Ivy-Schools-120657869.html.

38   Madej, Patricia. "Michael Cohen Testimony: Trump, a Wharton Alum, Told Me to Threaten Colleges to Not Release Grades." *Philadelphia Inquirer*, February 27, 2019. https://www.inquirer.com/politics/nation/michael-cohen-testimony -hearing-statement-trump-penn-wharton-fordham-20190227.html.

39   Fisher, Marc. "'Grab That Record': How Trump's High School Transcript Was Hidden." *The Washington Post*, March 5, 2019. https://www.washingtonpost.com/politics/grab-that-record-how-trumps -high-school-transcript-was-hidden/2019/03/05/8815b7b8-3c61-11e9-aaae -69364b2ed137_story.html.

40   Video, ABC News. "President Trump Has Called Himself Smart Six Times Before." *ABC News*, January 8, 2018. https://abcnews.go.com/Politics/ president-trump-called-smart-six-times-before/story?id=52209712.

41   Burleigh, Nina. "Trump Speaks at Fourth-Grade Level, Lowest of Last 15 U.S. Presidents, New Analysis Finds." *Newsweek*, February 26, 2019. https://www.newsweek.com/trump-fire-and-fury-smart-genius-obama -774169.

42   Hiltzik, Michael. "Column: Is This the Most 'Vicious' Thing Donald Trump Ever Did in Business?" *Los Angeles Times*, October 20, 2015. https://www.latimes.com/business/hiltzik/la-fi-mh-nastiest-thing-donald -trump-ever-did-20151020-column.html.

43   Kruse, Michael, Jeremy B. White, Sam Sutton and Carly Sitrin, and Bill Mahoney and Josh Gerstein. "The Man Who Beat Donald Trump." *POLITICO Magazine*, April 25, 2016. https://www.politico.com/magazine/story/2016/04/donald-trump-marvin -roffman-casino-lawsuit-213855.

44   Associated, Press. "Trump Taj Mahal Casino Sold for 4 Cents on the Dollar." *Los Angeles Times*, May 9, 2017. https://www.latimes.com/business/la-fi -trump-taj-mahal-20170509-story.html.

45   Ross, Janell. "Donald Trump's Doubling down on the Central Park Five Reflects a Bigger Problem." *The Washington Post*, October 8, 2016. https://www.washingtonpost.com/news/the-fix/wp/2016/10/08/donald -trumps-doubling-down-on-the-central-park-five-reflects-a-bigger-problem/.

46   Fahrenthold, David A. "Trump Recorded Having Extremely Lewd Conversation about Women in 2005." *The Washington Post,* October 8, 2016. https://www.washingtonpost.com/politics/trump-recorded-having -extremely-lewd-conversation-about-women-in-2005/2016/10/07/ 3b9ce776-8cb4-11e6-bf8a-3d26847eeed4_story.html

47   Victor, Daniel. "'Access Hollywood' Reminds Trump: 'The Tape Is Very Real'." *The New York Times,* November 28, 2017. https://www.nytimes.com/2017/ 11/28/us/politics/donald-trump-tape.html.

48   *Full Tape with Lewd Donald Trump Remarks (Access Hollywood). Access,* 2016. https://www.youtube.com/watch?v=NcZcTnykYbw.

49   Stableford, Dylan. "Trump Admits He Reimbursed Cohen for Stormy Daniels' Hush Money' Payment." Yahoo! News, May 3, 2018. https://news.yahoo.com/ trump-admits-reimbursed-cohen-stormy-daniels-hush-money-125017365. html.

50   Burke, Michael. "Fox News Killed Stormy Daniels Hush Money Report before Election: New Yorker." The Hill, March 4, 2019. https://thehill.com/ homenews/media/432430-fox-killed-stormy-daniels-hush-money-report- before-election-new-yorker.

Chapter 2

51   Silver, Nate. "Why FiveThirtyEight Gave Trump A Better Chance Than Almost Anyone Else." *FiveThirtyEight,* November 11, 2016. https://fivethirtyeight.com/features/why-fivethirtyeight-gave-trump-a -better-chance-than-almost-anyone-else/.

52   Silver, Nate. "The Comey Letter Probably Cost Clinton The Election." *FiveThirtyEight,* May 3, 2017. https://fivethirtyeight.com/features/the-comey -letter-probably-cost-clinton-the-election/.

53   Davis, Lanny J. *The Unmaking of the President: How FBI Director James Comey Cost Hillary Clinton the Presidency.* New York, NY: Scribner, an imprint of Simon & Schuster, Inc., 2018.

54   Emerson College. "Michigan 2016 Presidential Election Polls: Clinton vs. Trump." 270toWin.com, October 28, 2016. https://www.270towin.com/2016-polls-clinton-trump/michigan/.

55   Emerson College. "Wisconsin 2016 Presidential Election Polls: Clinton vs. Trump." 270toWin.com, October 29, 2016. https://www.270towin.com/2016-polls-clinton-trump/wisconsin/.

56   RealClearPolitics. "Election 2016 - Pennsylvania: Trump vs. Clinton." RealClearPolitics, November 1, 2016. https://www.realclearpolitics.com/ epolls/2016/president/pa/pennsylvania_trump_vs_clinton-5633.html.

57   Blake, Aaron. "How America Decided, at the Last Moment, to Elect Donald Trump." *The Washington Post*, November 17, 2016. https://www.washingtonpost.com/news/the-fix/wp/2016/11/17/ how-america-decided-at-the-very-last-moment-to-elect-donald-trump/.

58   Illing, Sean. "Did Trump's White House Staff Break the Law by Using Private Email? I Asked 7 Legal Experts." *Vox*, October 3, 2017. https://www.vox.com/ 2017/10/3/16384126/trump-white-house-private-email-kushner-bannon.

59   Miller, Greg. "State Department Probe of Clinton Emails Finds No Deliberate Mishandling of Classified Information." *The Washington Post*, October 18, 2019. https://www.washingtonpost.com/national-security/state-department -probe-of-clinton-emails-finds-no-deliberate-mishandling-of-classified -information/2019/10/18/83339446-f1dc-11e9-8693-f487e46784aa_story.html.

60   Miller, Greg, Greg Jaffe, and Philip Rucker. "How Trump's Skepticism of U.S. Intelligence on Russia Left an Election Threat Unchecked." *The Washington Post*, December 14, 2017. https://www.washingtonpost.com/graphics/2017/world/national-security/ donald-trump-pursues-vladimir-putin-russian-election-hacking/.

Chapter 3

61   Dann, Carrie. "Trump's Electoral College Win Was Not the Biggest Since Reagan." NBCNews.com, February 17, 2017. https://www.nbcnews.com/politics/donald-trump/trump-s-electoral-college -win-was-not-biggest-reagan-n722016.

62   Olsen, Matthew 12k, and Benjamin Haas. "'The Electoral College Is A National Security Threat': Liberal Politico Now Pushing For COLLAPSE." *Conservative Daily Post*, September 21, 2017. https://conservativedailypost.com/the-electoral-college-is-a-national -security-threat-liberal-politico-now-pushing-for-collapse/.

63   Talking Points. "The Electoral College: Should It Be Abolished?" *The Week Magazine*, April 5, 2019. https://theweek.com/magazine.

64   Blake, Aaron. "Analysis | Trump and Kobach Say Illegal Votes May Have given Clinton the Popular Vote. The Math Disagrees." *The Washington Post,* July 19, 2017. https://www.washingtonpost.com/news/the-fix/wp/2017/07/19/the-white-house-still-thinks-illegal-votes-may-have-given-clinton-the-popular-vote-basic-logic-and-math-disagree/?utm_term=.c0a1d431f8a0.

65   Lopez, Tomas, and Jennifer L. Clark. "Uncovering Kris Kobach's Anti-Voting History." Brennan Center for Justice, May 11, 2017. https://www.brennancenter.org/blog/uncovering-kris-kobach's-anti-voting-history.

66   Ingraham, Christopher. "Analysis | Federal Judge Upholds Fine against Kris Kobach for 'Pattern' of 'Misleading the Court' in Voter-ID Cases." *The Washington Post,* July 26, 2017. https://www.washingtonpost.com/news/wonk/wp/2017/07/26/federal-judge-upholds-fine-against-kris-kobach-for-pattern-of-misleading-the-court-in-voter-id-cases/?utm_term=.8a6b3081e963.

67   Dunlap, Matthew. "I'm on Trump's Voter Fraud Commission. I'm Suing It to Find out What It's Doing." *The Washington Post,* November 30, 2017. https://www.washingtonpost.com/outlook/im-on-trumps-voter-fraud-commission-im-suing-it-to-find-out-what-its-doing/2017/11/30/1034574c-d3b0-11e7-95bf-df7c19270879_story.html?utm_term=.17f5346fa72.

68   Palast, Greg, and Ted Ball. *The Best Democracy Money Can Buy: A Tale of Billionaires & Ballot Bandits.* New York, NY: Seven Stories Press, 2016.

69   McCann, Erin. "Who Is Registered to Vote in Two States? Some in Trump's Inner Circle." *The New York Times,* January 27, 2017. https://www.nytimes.com/2017/01/27/us/politics/trump-cabinet-family-voter-registration.html.

70   Wagner, John. "Trump Abolishes Controversial Commission Studying Alleged Voter Fraud." *The Washington Post,* January 4, 2018. https://www.washingtonpost.com/politics/trump-abolishes-controversial-commission-studying-voter-fraud/2018/01/03/665b1878-f0e2-11e7-b3bf-ab90a706e175_story.html?utm_term=.8275bce33d24.

71   Santa Cruz Indivisible. "What You Need to Know About Interstate Crosscheck Voting Software." Santa Cruz: Santa Cruz Indivisible, July 1, 2017.

72   Lopez, German. "Voter Suppression Didn't Cost Hillary Clinton the Election." *Vox,* November 11, 2016. https://www.vox.com/policy-and-politics/2016/11/11/13597452/voter-suppression-clinton-trump-2016.

73   Berman, Ari. "Rigged: How Voter Suppression Threw Wisconsin to Trump." *Mother Jones*, November, December, 2017. https://www.motherjones.com/politics/2017/10/voter-suppression-wisconsin-election-2016/.

74   Wines, Michael. "Some Republicans Acknowledge Leveraging Voter ID Laws for Political Gain." *The New York Times*, September 16, 2016. https://www.nytimes.com/2016/09/17/us/some-republicans-acknowledge-leveraging-voter-id-laws-for-political-gain.html.

75   Marley, Patrick, Jason Stein, and Bruce Vielmetti. "Federal Judge Strikes down Wisconsin's Voter ID Law." *Journal Sentinel*, April 29, 2014. http://archive.jsonline.com/news/statepolitics/federal-judge-strikes-down-wisconsins-voter-id-law-b99258822z1-257200321.html/.

76   Lee, Michelle. "Analysis | Do Voter ID Laws Help or Hurt Voter Turnout?" *The Washington Post*, May 30, 2017. https://www.washingtonpost.com/news/fact-checker/wp/2017/05/30/do-voter-id-laws-help-or-hurt-voter-turnout/.

77   Hasen, Rick. "Careful New Study Finds at Least Thousands in Two Wisconsin Counties Didn't Vote Because of Voter ID Requirements, Confusion Over Them." *Election Law Blog*, September 25, 2017. https://electionlawblog.org/.

78   Levine, Sam. "Thousands of Voters Didn't Cast A Ballot in Wisconsin Because Of Voter ID, Study Finds." *HuffPost*, September 27, 2017. https://www.huffpost.com/entry/wisconsin-voter-id_n_59ca6e60e4b01cc57ff5bdd5.

79   Associated Press. "Wisconsin Court Overturns Ruling That Ordered Voter Purge." *The Wall Street Journal*, February 28, 2020. https://www.wsj.com/articles/wisconsin-court-overturns-ruling-that-ordered-voter-purge-11582915847.

Chapter 4

80   Miller, Hayley. "Macedonian Teen Claims He Made $60,000 Producing Fake News During Election." *HuffPost*, December 9, 2016. https://www.huffpost.com/entry/macedonian-teen-claims-trump-supporters-paid-him-60k-to-produce-fake-news-during-campaign_n_584ac403e4b0bd9c3dfc51b7.L

81   Baker, Peter, and Eileen Sullivan. "Trump Accuses Mueller of a Personal Vendetta as Calls for Impeachment Grow." *The New York Times*, May 30, 2019. https://www.nytimes.com/2019/05/30/us/politics/trump-russia-help-elected.html.

82   Fritze, John, and Gregory Korte. "Trump Accepts Putin's Denials of Election Meddling, Prompting Outrage from Congress." *USA Today,* July 16, 2018. https://www.usatoday.com/story/news/politics/2018/07/16/vladimir-putin -denies-meddling-2016-presidential-election/788219002/.

83   Director of National Intelligence, and James R. Clapper, Assessing Russian Activities and Intentions in Recent U.S. Elections § (2017). https://www.dni.gov/files/documents/ICA_2017_01.pdf.

84   Howard, Philip, Bharath Ganesh, Dimitra Liotsiou, John Kelly, and Camille Francois. "The IRA, Social Media and Political Polarization in the United States, 2012-2018." Computational Research Project. University of Oxford and Graphika, January 23, 2019. https://comprop.oii.ox.ac.uk/wp-content/uploads/sites/93/2018/12/ The-IRA-Social-Media-and-Political-Polarization.pdf.

85   DiResta, Renee, Jonathan Albright, and Ben Johnson. "The Tactics & Tropes of the Internet Research Agency." *New Knowledge.* New Knowledge, Columbia University, and Canfield Research, November 8, 2018. https://int.nyt.com/data/documenthelper/533-read-report-internet -research-agency/7871ea6d5b7bedafbf19/optimized/full.pdf.

86   Liptak, Adam. "Supreme Court Blocks Release of Full Mueller Report for Now." *The New York Times,* May 20, 2020. https://www.nytimes. com/2020/05/20/us/supreme-court-blocks-mueller-report-release.html.

87   Cummings, William, Tom Vanden Brook, Kevin Johnson, and Bart Jansen. "Mueller's Investigation Is Done. Here Are the 34 People He Indicted along the Way." *USA Today,* March 25, 2019. https://www.usatoday.com/story/news/politics/2019/03/25/muellers -russia-report-special-counsel-indictments-charges/3266050002/.

88   Breaux, Harold J. "Fake News Elected Trump as President." Web log. *Complex Politics* (blog), January 6, 2017. https://complexpolitics.org/2017/01/06/fake-news-elected-trump/.

89   Breaux, Harold J. "Triple Whammy Tilted Electoral College to Trump." Web log. *Complex Politics* (blog), January 25, 2018. https://complexpolitics.org/2018/01/25/triple-whammy-tilted-electoral -college-to-trump/.

90   Watts, Clint. *Messing with the Enemy: Surviving in a Social Media World of Hackers, Terrorists, Russians and Fake News.* New York, NY: Harper, 2019

91   *NBER,* Hunt Allcott, and Matthew Gentzkow, Social Media and Fake News in the 2016 Election § (2017). https://www.nber.org/papers/w23089.

92   *NBER*, Hunt Allcott, and Matthew Gentzkow. Social Media and Fake News in the 2016 Election § (2017). https://www.nber.org/papers/w23089.

93   Allcott, Hunt, Matthew Gentzkow, and Chan Yu. "Trends in the Diffusion of Misinformation on Social Media." Stanford University. New York University, Microsoft Research, Stanford University, and NBER, October 2018. https://web.stanford.edu/~gentzkow/research/fake-news-trends.pdf.

94   Crawford, Krysten. "Stanford Study Examines Fake News and the 2016 Presidential Election." *Stanford News*. Stanford University, March 8, 2018. https://news.stanford.edu/2017/01/18/stanford-study-examines-fake-news -2016-presidential-election/.

95   Anderson, Monica. "Social Media Leads Some Users to Rethink a Political Issue." Pew Research Center, November 7, 2016. http://www.pewresearch.org/fact-tank/2016/11/07/social-media-causes -some-users-to-rethink-their-views-on.

96   Silverman, Craig, *BuzzFeed News*, "Most Americans Who See Fake News Believe It, New Survey Says" December 6, 2016, https://www.buzzfeed.com/ craigsilverman/fake-news-survey?utm_term=.ved04zr2a#.ijndz2KAW

97   Bershidsky, Leonid. "The Numbers Are In: Fake News Didn't Work." Bloomberg.com, January 23, 2017. https://www.bloomberg.com/opinion/ articles/2017-01-23/the-numbers-are-in-fake-news-didn-t-work.

98   Klein, Aaron. "Facebook 'Fact-Checker' Poynter: Worth Considering 'Fake News' Didn't Significantly Impact 2016 Election." *MixedTimes*, 2017. https://www.mixedtimes.com/news/facebook-fact-checker-poynter-worth -considering-fake-news-didnt-significantly-impact-2016-election.

99   Timberg, Craig. "Russian Propaganda May Have Been Shared Hundreds of Millions of Times, New Research Says." *The Washington Post*, October 5, 2017. https://www.washingtonpost.com/news/the-switch/wp/2017/10/05/russian -propaganda-may-have-been-shared-hundreds-of-millions-of-times-new -research-says/?utm.

100 Maremont, Mark, and Rob Barry. "Russian Twitter Support for Trump Began Right After He Started Campaign." *The Wall Street Journal*, November 6, 2017. https://www.wsj.com/articles/russian-twitter-support-for-trump-began -right-after-he-started-campaign-1509964380.

101 O'Sullivan, Donnie, and Laurie Segall. "Twitter Misses Senate Deadline on Russian Meddling." *CNNMoney*, January 9, 2018. https://money.cnn.com/ 2018/01/09/media/twitter-russia-senate-intelligence-committee-questions/ index.html.

102 Karpf, David. "Analysis | People Are Hyperventilating over a Study of Russian Propaganda on Facebook. Just Breathe Deeply." *The Washington Post,* October 12, 2017. https://www.washingtonpost.com/news/monkey-cage/wp/2017/10/12/people-are-hyperventilating-over-a-new-study-of-russian-propaganda-on-facebook-just-breathe-deeply/.

103 McMillan, Robert. "New Report Points to How Russian Misinformation May Have Adapted Since 2016 Election." *The Wall Street Journal,* June 16, 2020. https://www.wsj.com/articles/russia-linked-disinformation-campaign-spread-messages-across-multiple-platforms-to-elude-detection-new-report-says-11592319829.

104 Lapowsky, Issie. "Shadow Politics: Meet the Digital Sleuth Exposing Fake News." *Wired,* July 17, 2018. https://www.wired.com/story/shadow-politics-meet-the-digital-sleuth-exposing-fake-news/.

105 Olson, Laura. "Pennsylvania Turns up Several Times in the Redacted Mueller Report." *The Morning Call,* April 18, 2019. https://www.mcall.com/news/pennsylvania/capitol-ideas/mc-nws-pa-mueller-report-trump-russia-pennsylvania-rallies-20190418-6apqesaatvesjoy4uuymxujnv4-story.html.

106 Mueller, Robert S., and Alan M. Dershowitz. *The Mueller Report: The Final Report of the Special Counsel into Donald Trump, Russia, and Collusion.* New York, NY: Skyhorse Publishing, 2019.

107 Raju, Manu, Dylan Byers, and Dana Bash. "Exclusive: Russian-Linked Facebook Ads Targeted Michigan, Wisconsin." *CNN,* October 4, 2017. https://www.cnn.com/2017/10/03/politics/russian-facebook-ads-michigan-wisconsin/index.html.

Chapter 5

108 Cohen, Moss. "Business News." *CnnMoney,* April 27, 2017. https://money.cnn.com/video/news/2017/04/27/obama-mocks-trump-correspondents-dinner.cnnmoney/index.html.

109 Glasser, Susan B. "'Obamagate' Is Niche Programming for Trump Superfans." *The New Yorker,* May 15, 2020. https://www.newyorker.com/news/letter-from-trumps-washington/obamagate-is-niche-programming-for-trump-superfans.

110 Rubin, Jennifer. "Opinion | McConnell Owes the Country a Fuller Explanation on Russian Meddling." *The Washington Post*, February 20, 2018. https://www.washingtonpost.com/blogs/right-turn/wp/2018/02/20/mcconnell-owes-the-country-a-fuller-explanation-on-russian-meddling/.

111 Kiely, Eugene. "Michael Flynn's Russia Timeline." FactCheck.org, August 10, 2018. https://www.factcheck.org/2017/12/michael-flynns-russia-timeline/.

112 Barber, C. Ryan. "Thousands of Ex-Prosecutors Urge Flynn Judge to Question Barr's Move to Drop Case." *National Law Journal*, May 11, 2020. https://www.law.com/nationallawjournal/2020/05/11/thousands-of-ex-prosecutors-urge-flynn-judge-to-question-barrs-move-to-drop-case/?slreturn=20200713192713.

113 Associated Press. "Q&A: What Does 'Unmasking' Someone in an Intel Report Mean?" *U.S. News & World Report*, May 14, 2020. https://www.usnews.com/news/politics/articles/2020-05-13/q-a-what-does-unmasking-someone-in-an-intel-report-mean.

114 Olson, Tyler, and Brooke Singman. "Trump Weighs in on Unmasking: 'Greatest Political Crime in the History of Our Country'." *Fox News*, May 14, 2020. https://www.foxnews.com/politics/trump-weighs-in-on-flynn.

115 Savage, Charlie. "N.S.A. 'Unmaskings' of U.S. Identities Soared Last Year, Report Says." *The New York Times*, April 30, 2019. https://www.nytimes.com/2019/04/30/us/politics/nsa-unmaskings-surveillance-report.html.

116 Forgey, Quint, and Josh Gerstein. "Barr Throws Cold Water on Trump's 'Obamagate' Campaign." *POLITICO*, May 19, 2020. https://www.politico.com/news/2020/05/18/barr-trump-obamagate-265037.

117 Macias, Amanda. "Trump Accuses Barr of Double Standard for Saying It's Unlikely DOJ Will Prosecute Obama, Biden." *CNBC*, May 18, 2020. https://www.cnbc.com/2020/05/18/obama-biden-criminal-investigation-unlikely-attorney-general-barr-says.html.

118 Gerstein, Josh, and Kyle Cheney. "'Everything about This Is Irregular': Ex-Judge Tapped to Review Flynn Case Blasts Trump DOJ." *POLITICO*, June 10, 2020. https://www.politico.com/news/2020/06/10/gleeson-flynn-sullivan-barr-justice-department-311018.

119 Williams, Juan. "Juan Williams: Trump's Dangerous Insecurity about Obama." *The Hill*, September 9, 2019. https://thehill.com/opinion/white-house/460402-juan-williams-trumps-dangerous-insecurity-about-obama.

120 Stein, Sam. "Robert Draper Book: GOP Leadership Plotted to Make Obama a One-Termer the Night of His Inauguration." *HuffPost*, August 10, 2014. https://www.huffpost.com/entry/robert-draper-anti-obama-campaign_n_1452899.

121 Raju, Manu. "McConnell's Plan to Halt Obama." *POLITICO*, August 20, 2014. https://www.politico.com/story/2014/08/2014-election-mitch-mcconnells-barack-obama-confrontation-110154.

122 Gomez, Amanda Michelle. "Trump Says He'll Announce a 'Phenomenal' New Health Care Plan Soon. Where Was It the Last 2 Years?" *ThinkProgress*, June 17, 2019. https://archive.thinkprogress.org/trump-announce-phenomenal-new-health-care-plan-b509b7b1844f/.

123 Waldman, Paul. "Opinion | Why William Barr Wants the GOP to Stop Trying to Destroy Obamacare." *The Washington Post*, May 5, 2020. https://www.washingtonpost.com/opinions/2020/05/05/why-william-barr-wants-gop-stop-trying-destroy-obamacare/.

124 United Nations. "Paris Agreement: Essential Elements." United Nations Climate Change, December 12, 2015. https://unfccc.int/process-and-meetings/the-paris-agreement/the-paris-agreement.

125 Popovich, Nadja, Livia Albeck-ripka, and Kendra Pierre-Louis. "The Trump Administration Is Reversing 100 Environmental Rules. Here's the Full List." *The New York Times*, June 2, 2019. https://www.nytimes.com/interactive/2020/climate/trump-environment-rollbacks.html.

126 Lombardo, Crystal. "Environmental Impact of Deepwater Horizon Oil Spill." *Vision Launch Media*, January 14, 2017. https://visionlaunch.com/environmental-impact-deepwater-horizon-oil-spill/.

127 Davenport, Coral. "Interior Dept. Loosens Offshore-Drilling Safety Rules Dating from Deepwater Horizon." *The New York Times*, May 2, 2019. https://www.nytimes.com/2019/05/02/climate/offshore-drilling-safety-rollback-deepwater-horizon.html.

128 Folley, Aris. "Trump Says 'Air and Water Are the Cleanest They've Ever Been' in US." *The Hill*, June 21, 2019. https://thehill.com/policy/energy-environment/449239-trump-says-air-and-water-are-the-cleanest-theyve-ever-been-before.

129 "Chesapeake Bay." *Wikipedia*, July 25, 2020. https://en.wikipedia.org/wiki/Chesapeake_Bay.

130 Hutzell, Rick. "Maryland, Chesapeake Bay Foundation, Anne Arundel Say They'll Sue EPA over Failure to Enforce Cleanup Goals." *Capital Gazette*, May 18, 2020. https://www.capitalgazette.com/environment/ac-cn -chesapeake-bay-lawsuit-20200518-qpndtaknljb4xn2tailmoi4rpe-story.html.

131 Colias, Mike, Ben Foldy, and Andrew Restuccia. "The Auto Industry Wanted Easier Environmental Rules. It Got Chaos." *The Wall Street Journal*, February 3, 2020. https://www.wsj.com/articles/the-auto-industry-wanted-easier -environmental-rules-it-got-chaos-11580745826.

Chapter 6

132 Glenn Kessler, Salvador Rizzo. "Analysis | President Trump Made 18,000 False or Misleading Claims in 1,170 Days." *The Washington Post*, April 14, 2020. https://www.washingtonpost.com/politics/2020/04/14/ president-trump-made-18000-false-or-misleading-claims-1170-days/.

133 Leonhardt, David. "Donald Trump vs. the United States of America." *The New York Times*, September 22, 2019. https://www.nytimes.com/2019/09/22/ opinion/trump-ukraine-whistle-blower.html.

134 Johnston, Nicholas. "How 9 'Art of the Deal' Quotes Explain the Trump Presidency." *Axios*, December 15, 2017. https://www.axios.com/how-9-art-of -the-deal-quotes-explain-the-trump-presidency-1513300122-183eaed4-4c48 -4527-a7ed-c57dd143865a.html.

135 "Rudy Giuliani Contradicts Trump, Says the President Knew about Michael Cohen's $130,000 Payment to Stormy Daniels and Reimbursed Cohen for It." *Business Insider*, May 2, 2018. https://www.businessinsider.com/did-trump -pay-stormy-daniels-michael-cohen-rudy-giuliani-2018-5.

136 Abrams, Abigail. "Sean Spicer Regrets Comments on Inauguration Crowd Size." *Time*, January 4, 2018. https://time.com/5088900/sean-spicer -screwed-up-inauguration-hitler/.

137 Hasen, Richard L. "Opinion | Trump Is Wrong about the Dangers of Absentee Ballots." *The Washington Post*, April 9, 2020. https://www.washingtonpost.com/ opinions/2020/04/09/trump-is-wrong-about-dangers-absentee-ballots/.

138 Williams, Pete. "Appeals Court, in Blow to Kobach, Strikes down Kansas Law Requiring Proof of Citizenship to Vote." *NBCNews.com*, April 30, 2020. https://www.nbcnews.com/politics/politics-news/appeals-court-blow -kobach-strikes-down-kansas-law-requiring-proof-n1195511.

139 Ura, Alexa. "Someone did not do their due diligence" *The Texas Tribune*, February 1, 2019 https://www.sacurrent.com/the-daily/archives/2019/02/01/someone-did-not-do-their-due-diligence-how-an-attempt-to-review-texas-voter-rolls-turned-into-a-debacle

140 Gardner, Amy, and Dawsey, Josh. "Trump Escalates Campaign to Discredit Mail Balloting, Threatening Federal Funds to Two Battleground States." *The Washington Post*, May 20, 2020. https://www.washingtonpost.com/politics/trump-threatens-funding-for-michigan-nevada-over-absentee-mail-in-voting-plans/2020/05/20/2f86d078-9aa2-11ea-ac72-3841fcc9b35f_story.html.

141 Nix, Naomi, and Bloomberg. "Amazon Says They Lost a $10 Billion DoD Contract Because Trump Sees Bezos as a 'Political Enemy'." *Fortune*, December 9, 2019. https://fortune.com/2019/12/09/amazon-pentagon-cloud-contract-trump-bezos/.

142 Patacca, Gina. "Letter: Problems with Post Office Extend beyond Amazon." *The Columbus Dispatch*, April 28, 2020. https://www.dispatch.com/opinion/20200428/letter-problems-with-post-office-extend-beyond-amazon.

143 Goldblatt, Daniel. "Trump Calls ABC News' Jonathan Karl a 'Third-Rate Reporter' During Monday Briefing (Video)." *Yahoo!*, April 7, 2020. https://sg.style.yahoo.com/trump-calls-abc-news-jonathan-015409065.html.

144 Goldberg, Jonah. "Trump's Daily Coronavirus Briefings Shine Light on His Inadequacy: COMMENTARY." *Baltimore Sun*, April 1, 2020. https://www.baltimoresun.com/opinion/op-ed/bs-ed-op-0405-trump-daily-briefing-inadequacy-20200402-t2m6mcoywnbotfuhf4dz2cnuzu-story.html.

145 Milbank, Dana. "Opinion | 'I Believe I Am Treated Worse,' Trump Says. As If." *The Washington Post*, May 5, 2020. https://www.washingtonpost.com/opinions/2020/05/05/i-believe-i-am-treated-worse-trump-says-as-if/.

146 Moreau, Jordan. "Trump Calls for Investigation into Unfounded Joe Scarborough Murder Conspiracy." *Variety*, May 24, 2020. https://variety.com/2020/biz/news/trump-joe-scarborough-murder-conspiracy-theory-1234615269/.

147 Baker, Peter, and Katie Benner. "Contradicting Trump, Barr Says Bunker Visit Was for Safety, Not an 'Inspection'." *The New York Times*, June 9, 2020. https://www.nytimes.com/2020/06/08/us/politics/barr-trump-bunker-george-floyd.html.

148 Fang, Marina. "Trump Floats Conspiracy That 75-Year-Old Buffalo Protester Pushed by Police Was 'A Set Up'." *Yahoo!*, June 9, 2020. https://www.yahoo.com/huffpost/trump-buffalo-protester-conspiracy-125552760.html.

149 Amadeo, Kimberly. "Why Tariffs Raise Prices." *The Balance*, October 27, 2019. https://www.thebalance.com/tariff-pros-cons-and-examples-3305967.

150 Werschkul, Ben. "Trump Made This False Claim about China and Tariffs at Least 108 Times in 2019." *Yahoo!* Finance, December 27, 2019. https://finance. yahoo.com/news/trump-has-made-this-false-claim-about-china-and-tariffs -at-least-100-times-182318319.html.

151 Wise, Justin. "Kudlow Contradicts Trump, Says US Will Also Take Hit from China Tariffs." *The Hill*, May 13, 2019. https://thehill.com/homenews/ administration/443295-kudlow-contradicts-trump-says-china-isnt-paying -tariffs-on-goods.

152 Reich, Robert. "Robert Reich: Trump's 4 Biggest Lies about Today's Economy." *Salon*, September 18, 2018. https://www.salon.com/2018/09/17/ robert-reich-trumps-4-biggest-lies-about-todays-economy_partner/.

153 Singer, Emily. "Trump Farm Bailout Costs More than Double the Auto Bailout That GOP Slammed." *The American Independent*, December 2, 2019. https://americanindependent.com/donald-trump-farming-bailouts-trade -war-china-barack-obama-auto-industry-cars/.

154 *Wikipedia.* "Lawrence Hogan." *Wikipedia*, July 30, 2020. https://en.wikipedia. org/wiki/Lawrence_Hogan.

155 *Wikipedia.* "List of Nicknames Used by Donald Trump." *Wikipedia*, August 13, 2020. https://en.wikipedia.org/wiki/List_of_nicknames used_by_Donald _Trump.

Chapter 7

156 Rucker, Philip, and Carol Leonnig. *A Very Stable Genius: Donald J. Trump's Testing of America.* London, UK: Bloomsbury Publishing, 2020.

157 Barnes, Julian E., and Adam Goldman. "For Spy Agencies, Briefing Trump Is a Test of Holding His Attention." *The New York Times*, May 21, 2020. https://www.nytimes.com/2020/05/21/us/politics/presidents-daily-brief -trump.html.

158 Moran, Lee. "George Conway Taunts Trump with A Long List of His Geopolitical Gaffes." *HuffPost*, January 29, 2020. https://www.huffpost.com/entry/george-conway-donald-trump -geopolitical-gaffes_n_5e3135dbc5b6cd99e785d22f.

159 Hellmann, Jessie. "Trump Demands Governors Allow Churches to Open." *The Hill*, May 22, 2020. https://thehill.com/homenews/administration/499184-trump-demands-governors-allow-churches-to-open.

160 Fink, Jenni, and Naveed Jamali. "Exclusive: Defense Department Expects Coronavirus Will 'Likely' Become Global Pandemic in 30 Days, as Trump Strikes Serious Tone." *Newsweek*, March 1, 2020. http://www.newsweek.com/coronavirus-department-defense-pandemic-30-days-1489876.

161 *Thirteen Days*. Wikipedia, 2017. https://en.wikipedia.org/wiki/Thirteen_Days_.

162 Brower, Kate Andersen. "Trump's Contempt for the Ex-Presidents Is Costing Us Right Now." *The New York Times*, April 27, 2020. https://www.nytimes.com/2020/04/27/opinion/coronavirus-trump-presidents.html.

163 Mangan, Dan. "Trump Dismissed Coronavirus Pandemic Worry in January—Now Claims He Long Warned about It." *CNBC*, March 18, 2020. https://www.cnbc.com/2020/03/17/trump-dissed-coronavirus-pandemic-worry-now-claims-he-warned-about-it.html.

164 Stevens, Harry, and Shelley Tan. "These Quotes Show How Trump's Response to the Coronavirus Has Changed over Time." *The Washington Post*, March 31, 2020. https://www.washingtonpost.com/graphics/2020/politics/trump-coronavirus-statements/.

165 Leonhardt, David. "A Complete List of Trump's Attempts to Play Down Coronavirus." *The New York Times*, March 15, 2020. https://www.nytimes.com/2020/03/15/opinion/trump-coronavirus.html.

166 Lipton, Eric, David E. Sanger, Maggie Haberman, et al. "He Could Have Seen What Was Coming: Behind Trump's Failure on the Virus." *The New York Times*, April 11, 2020. https://www.nytimes.com/2020/04/11/us/politics/coronavirus-trump-response.html.

167 Rein, Lisa. "Trump Replaces HHS Watchdog Who Found 'Severe Shortages' at Hospitals Combating Coronavirus." *Stars and Stripes*, May 3, 2020. https://www.stripes.com/news/us/trump-replaces-hhs-watchdog-who-found-severe-shortages-at-hospitals-combating-coronavirus-1.628289.

168 Millhiser, Ian. "Trump Tells a Nation Terrified of Coronavirus That None of This Is His Fault." *Vox*, March 13, 2020. https://www.vox.com/2020/3/13/21179119/trump-not-my-fault-coronavirus-press-conference.

169 Hendershot, Heather. "Perspective | The Truth about Trump's Uncle and What It Means for His Presidency." *The Washington Post*, March 12, 2020. https://www.washingtonpost.com/outlook/2020/03/12/truth-about-trumps-uncle-what-it-means-his-presidency/.

170 Boot, Max. "Opinion | The Worst President. Ever." *The Washington Post*, April 5, 2020. https://www.washingtonpost.com/opinions/2020/04/05/worst-president-ever/.

171 Biesecker, Michael. "US 'Wasted' Months before Preparing for Coronavirus Pandemic." *AP NEWS*, April 5, 2020. https://apnews.com/090600c299a8cf07f5b44d92534856bc.

172 Board, Baltimore Sun Editorial. "Anthony Fauci Is the Person of the Hour - so, Naturally, He's Also a Target: COMMENTARY." *Baltimore Sun*, April 8, 2020. https://www.baltimoresun.com/opinion/editorial/bs-ed-0407-fauci-death-threats-leadership-20200406-72p4gmainrh45gdoyfqk2mousa-story.html.

173 Falk, William. "Calling Dr. Fauci." *The Week*, April 6, 2020. https://www.theweek.com/articles/906409/calling-dr-fauci.

174 Parker, Ashley, Yasmeen Abutaleb, and Lena H. Sun. "Squandered Time—How the Trump Administration Lost Control of the Coronavirus Crisis." *The Washington Post*, March 8, 2020. https://www.msn.com/en-us/news/politics/squandered-time-how-the-trump-administration-lost-control-of-the-coronavirus-crisis/ar-BB10SJJJ.

175 Costa, Robert and Philip Rucker. "From Tweet Eruptions to Economic Steps, Trump Struggles for Calm amid Market Meltdown and Coronavirus Crisis." *The Washington Post*, March 10, 2020. https://www.washingtonpost.com/politics/trump-struggles-to-calm-nation-amid-market-meltdown-and-coronavirus-crisis/2020/03/09/6958ac90-6217-11ea-acca-80c22bbee96f_story.html.

176 Stieb, Matt. "Trump's Coronavirus Economic Council Was a Disaster Before It Began." *Intelligencer*, April 16, 2020. https://nymag.com/intelligencer/2020/04/trumps-covid-19-economic-council-was-a-mess-before-it-began.html.

177 Goddard, Taegan. "Has Anyone Found Trump's Soul?" *Political Wire*, April 6, 2020. https://politicalwire.com/2020/04/06/has-anyone-found-trumps-soul/.

178 Alonso-Zaldivar, Ricardo. "Trump's Disdain for 'Obamacare' Could Hamper Virus Response." *U.S. News & World Report*, April 13, 2020. https://www.usnews.com/news/business/articles/2020-04-13/trumps-disdain-for-obamacare-could-hamper-virus-response.

179 Glanz, James, and Campbell Robertson. "Lockdown Delays Cost at Least 36,000 Lives, Data Show." *The New York Times,* May 20, 2020. https://www.nytimes.com/2020/05/20/us/coronavirus-distancing-deaths. html.

180 Samuels, Brett. "Trump Calls Study on Taking Earlier Action against Coronavirus a 'Political Hit Job'." *The Hill,* May 21, 2020. https://thehill.com/homenews/administration/498985-trump-calls -columbia-study-showing-effects-of-earlier-coronavirus.

181 Collins, Gail, and Bret Stephens. "Donald Trump, Unmasked." *The New York Times,* May 12, 2020. https://www.nytimes.com/2020/05/12/opinion/ coronavirus-trump-masks.html.

182 Millhiser, Ian. "Trump Claims He Will 'Override the Governors' Who Closed Churches in the Pandemic." *Vox,* May 22, 2020. https://www.vox.com/2020/5/ 22/21267856/trump-churches-override-governors-not-legal-constitution -coronavirus.

183 Rucker, Philip. "Trump's Week of Retreat: The President Reverses Course as the Coronavirus Surges out of Control." *The Washington Post,* July 25, 2020. https://www.washingtonpost.com/politics/trumps-week-of-retreat-the -president-reverses-course-as-the-coronavirus-surges-out-of-control/2020/ 07/24/bf680c2c-cdc2-11ea-91f1-28aca4d833a0_story.html.

184 Upright, Ed, and Melissa Macaya. "July 23 Coronavirus News." *CNN,* July 24, 2020. https://www.cnn.com/world/live-news/coronavirus -pandemic-07-23-20-intl/index.html.

185 Erdman, Shelby Lin, Jacqueline Howard, Jen Christensen, and Katia Hetter. "Shut down the Country Again to Contain Covid-19, US Medical Experts Urge." *CNN,* July 24, 2020. https://www.cnn.com/2020/07/23/health/ shutdown-us-contain-coronavirus-wellness/index.html.